Concise Thesaurus

Concise Thesaurus

Taniya Sachdeva

PRABHAT
PAPERBACKS

Published by
PRABHAT PAPERBACKS
4/19 Asaf Ali Road,
New Delhi-110 002 (INDIA)
e-mail: prabhatbooks@gmail.com

ISBN 978-93-5266-644-7
Concise Thesaurus
by Taniya Sachdeva

Edition
First, 2018

Price
₹ 175.00 (Rupees One Hundred Seventy Five only)

Printed at
R-Tech Offset Printers, Delhi

Dedicated to the love
and
support of my family

Contents

aback (adv.)
surprisingly, suddenly, backwards, unexpectedly, unwarily
I was taken aback by her response.

abandon (v.)
desert, resign, forgo, relinquish, leave, vacate, quit, forsake, give up
One should not abandon anyone in desperate times.

abase (v.)
mortify, demean, downsize, degrade, humiliate, debase, disgrace, dishonour
We have heard so much about people abasing themselves before others for money.

abash (v.)
bewilder, daunt, embarrass, mortify, chagrin, discompose, humble, overawe, confound, disconcert, humiliate, shame, confuse, dishearten
The ignorants are abashed at the learning of the wise.

abate (v.)
die away, decrease, ease, diminish, relieve, slacken, lower, fade, decline
He abated the nuisance created by some miscreants.

abbreviate (v.)
contract, shorten, condense, abridge, reduce, cut, foreshorten, compress
I like to abbreviate words when I text on the mobile phone.

abduct (v.)
kidnap, snatch, seize, shanghai, capture
Nowadays, abducting has become so common that one has to be extremely careful all the time.

aberrant (adj.)
abnormal, errant,

divergent, odd, atypical, peculiar
We see some aberrant streaks in his behaviour.

abet (v.)
advocate, countenance, incite, sanction, aid, embolden, instigate, support, assist, encourage, promote, uphold
A priest would not incite to abet a crime.

abhor (v.)
detest, hate, despise, loathe, shudder at, nauseate
Dr. Frankenstein abhorred his creation.

abide (v.)
anticipate, dwell, remain, stop, await, endure, bear, expect, rest, tolerate, bide, inhabit, sojourn, wait, watch, continue
One is expected to abide by the rules.

ability (n.)
capacity, expertise, skill, aptitude, skill, competence
It is within his ability to give up lying.

abjure (v.)
retract, withdraw, reject formally, renounce, abstain from
Later on, in the court, he abjured his statement.

ablaze (adj.)
blazing, burning, flaming, on fire, afire, conflagrant, ignited, enflamed
I saw her visage all ablaze with happiness.

able (adj.)
capable, competent, fit, qualified, proficient, talented
She would be able to cope with the pressures at work.

abnormal (adj.)
deviant, odd, peculiar, exceptional, exceeding, freak, rare, unusual
For some reason, he was behaving in an abnormal way.

abode (n.)
home, house, domicile, dwelling, hearth, lodging, residence, roof
The abode of the Almighty is sacred, and should not be taken lightly.

abolish (v.)
annul, destroy, eliminate, nullify, obliterate,

invalidate, negate, dissolve
Apartheid was abolished for its inhuman practices aimed towards the coloured people.

abominable (adj.)
contemptible, detestable, hateful, loathsome, repugnant, obnoxious, unpleasant, disagreeable
This is such an abominable weather.

abomination (n.)
abhorrence, curse, hatred, plague, abuse, detestation, horror, shame, annoyance, disgust, iniquity, villainy, evil, nuisance
For Dr. Frankenstein, his creation was an abomination.

aboriginal (adj.)
domestic, local, native, indigenous, primordial
Africa has its share of aboriginal forests.

abort (v.)
abandon, annul, cancel, drop, recall, revoke, scrap
The mission has to be aborted immediately.

abound (v.)
brim, burst, crawl, overflow, swarm, teem
There is a venture in which opportunities abound.

about (adv.)
directing to, referencing, regarding, almost, close
It all happened about a year ago.

above (adv.)
atop, aloft, beyond, preeminent, overhead, superior, surpassing
These stairs will lead us to the rooms above.

abrasive (adj.)
corrosive, erosive, coarse, caustic, unsympathetic, inconsiderate, exasperating, maddening
He has suffered only because of his abrasive manners.

abreast (adj., adv.)
familiar, aligned, apprised, against, acquainted, informed
She always keeps abreast of the news.

abridgement (n.)
abbreviation, compend, summary, abstract, compendium, outline,

synopsis, analysis, digest
We are looking for an abridgement of this classic.

abrogate (v.)
revoke, annul, nullify, retract, withdraw, scrap, vacate, roll back
The Indian government policies can be abrogated on the basis of their legality.

abrupt (adj.)
quick, blunt, brusque, sudden, unexpected, curt
To our utter shock, the movie had an abrupt ending.

abscond (v.)
escape, flee, disappear, run off, break out
The criminal was trying to abscond from the scene of crime.

absence (n.)
lack, dearth, deficiency, need, truancy, want
The absence of students led to the cancellation of this seminar.

absolute (adj.)
definite, faultless, ideal, arbitrary, unconditional, whole, complete, total
There is no such thing as the absolute truth.

absolve (v.)
clear, exonerate, release, free from, vindicate, acquit, excuse, exculpate, liberate
She was absolved of her sins after the holy ceremony.

absorb (v.)
assimilate, consume, devour, engulf, learn, educate, sense, acquire, soak up
The sponge absorbed all the spilled water.

abstain (v.)
refrain, shun, avoid, forgo
One should abstain from abusive activities.

abstinence (n.)
frugality, self-denial, sobriety, continence, moderation, self-restraint, temperance
Abstinence in relation to some issues is encouraged in our society.

abstract (adj.)
obscure, profound, conceptual, ideal, special,

difficult, abstruse, detached, metaphysical
It is an abstract painting; it is cumbersome to put one's head around it.

abstracted (adj.)
absent, heedless, listless, preoccupied, absent-minded, inattentive, negligent, thoughtless, absorbed, indifferent
Philips is known for his abstracted stares.

abstruse (adj.)
difficult, complex, intricate, complicated, nuanced, profound, deep
The abstruse discourse was hard to keep up with.

absurd (adj.)
inane, ludicrous, ridiculous, foolish, silly, unreasonable, incongruous
What happened there was completely absurd.

abundant (adj.)
abound, plentiful, prolific, teeming, copious, generous, ample, aplenty
This dish is abundant with all the nutrients.

abuse (n.)
invective, vituperation, maltreat, manhandle, misuse, desecration, violation, condemnation
She abused her kids at multiple levels.

abyss (n.)
chasm, gorge, gulf, hole, ocean
I peeked down at the gaping abyss.

academic (adj.)
learned, erudite, literary, scholastic, intellectual, educational
He was always more interested in academic matters.

academy (n.)
school, college, academe, conservatory, seminary
This is the finest academy of literature in town.

accede (v.)
agree, allow, comply, grant, permit, sanction, consent, subscribe
Walt finally acceded to their demands.

accelerate (v.)
hasten, expedite, quicken, increase, boom, escalate, rise
Jim accelerated when he saw his competitor catching up with him.

accept (v.)
take, hold, maintain, embrace, conclude, have, to endure
Nancy accepted all the proposals that were presented in front of her.

accessible (adj.)
attainable, available, reachable, obtainable, open, affordable
The real estate is making homes accessible for the common man.

accessory (n.)
abettor, associate, companion, accomplice, attendant, participator, ally, partner, assistant, colleague
Tim Ford is the real partner; Susan is just an accessory.

accident (n.)
casualty, mischance, misadventure, misfortune, mishap
The child met with an accident due to his carelessness.

acclaim (n.)
applaud, praise, accolades, approval, kudos, distinction
The critics have acclaimed his performing skills in his recent movie.

acclimatize (v.)
adapt, adjust, accommodate, fit, acclimate
It takes at least to get acclimatised to difficult terrains.

accommodate (v.)
adapt, adjust, contain, conform, fit
It is better to accommodate rather than be a non-conformist.

accompany (v.)
chaperon, escort, follow, usher, supplement, attend, company
The father accompanied his daughter to her wedding chapel.

accomplice (n.)
abettor, accessary, cohort, confederate, partner, affiliate
Jesse was an accomplice in all the crimes Walt committed.

accomplish (v.)
achieve, attain, get, succeed, complete, do, fulfill, perform, carry out
Mahatma Gandhi accomplished feats

during the Indian freedom struggle.

accord (n.)
agreement, conformity, harmony, peace, treaty, convention
All the facts accord with the proposed theory.

account (n.)
anecdote, chronicle, history, narrative, record, story
We should also pay attention to the discrepancy in the criminal's accounts.

accumulate (v.)
collect, gather, cumulate, accrue, heap, store, burgeon
Some people are obsessive about accumulating money.

accusation (n.)
allegation, charge, complaint, indictment, slur
Micheal threw accusations at the face of Martha.

accustom (v.)
acquaint, familiarise, initiate, orientate, habituate
One should get accustomed to the new set-up before taking the plunge.

ace (n.)
master, champion, veteran, specialist, expert
He is a flute ace.

acerbic (adj.)
sarcastic, bitter, coarse, sharp, barbed, acrid, sardonic
Oscar has a habit of passing acerbic remarks.

ache (n.)
pain, sting, hurt, agony, pang
Toulose suffers from chronic headaches.

acknowledge (v.)
admit, agree, concede, grant, own up to, recognise
To acknowledge one's mistakes needs conscience.

acme (n.)
apex, peak, pinnacle, top, zenith, summit
Microsoft Corporation has reached the acme of excellence.

acquaintance (n.)
association, experience, fellowship, intimacy,

companionship, familiarity, friendship
People are happy to make acquaintance of important people.

acrimony (n.)
acerbity, harshness, severity, tartness, asperity, malignity, sharpness, unkindness, bitterness, moroseness
Sheila always criticises with an extra dash of acrimony.

act (v.)
execute, movement, exercise, operation, action, exertion, performance, consummation, exploit, proceeding, deed, feat, transaction, doing, motion, work
An act can have several repercussions.

active (n.)
agile, energetic, officious, sprightly, alert, expeditious, prompt, spry, brisk, industrious, quick, supple, bustling, lively, ready, vigorous
Christine is an active woman. She can juggle several things at a time.

acumen (n.)
acuteness, insight, perspicacity, sharpness, cleverness, keenness, discernment, sagacity, sharpness
In the arena of Humanities, we test the critical acumen of the students.

add (v.)
adjoin, annex, augment, extend, make up, affix, append, cast up, increase, subjoin, amplify, attach, enlarge, join on, sum up
Sometimes, people in general add insult to injury unknowingly.

addicted (adj.)
abandoned, devoted, given over, inclined, accustomed, disposed, given up, prone, attached, given, habituated, wedded
Almost one-third of our world is addicted to one thing or another.

address (v.)
cost, approach, hail, speak to, salute, woo, appeal, greet
In the court of law, it is imperative that we

address the judge with due respect.

address (n.)
discretion, manners, readiness, courtesy, ingenuity, politeness, tact, dexterity
The manner of address is a component which is to be used carefully in front of important people.

adequate (adj.)
able, competent, satisfactory, adapted, equal, fitting, sufficient, capable, commensurate, qualified, suitable
The number of plates and glasses should be adequate for Nikita's family function.

adherent (n.)
aid, ally, disciple, aider, backer, follower, partisan
Nazism had witnessed many ardent adherents of Hitler.

adhesive (n.)
cohesive, gummy, sticky, glutinous, sticking, viscous
Fevicol is one of the most used adhesives around the world.

adjacent (adj.)
abutting, neighboring, adjoining, close, coterminous, next, attached, conterminous, near, beside
I think that those two friends have adjacent rooms.

admire (v.)
adore, delight in, extol, respect, venerate, applaud, enjoy, love, honor, revere, wonder
I admire people who have humanitarian instinct.

adorn (v.)
beautify, decorate, embellish, garnish, illustrate, bedeck, gild, ornament, deck
The mother had adorned the room for her boy's birthday celebration.

affront (v.)
exasperate, offend, vex, annoy, insult, provoke, displease, wound
Sophie was going to affront Max for the discomfort he had caused her.

agent (n.)
actor, factor, means,

operator, doer, instrument, performer
There are many corrupt agents at play in every system.

agree (v.)
accede, admit, accept, approve, consent, concede, accord, assent, comply, harmonise
Margaret Thatcher agreed to the entrepreneurial British world to save the British economy.

agriculture (n.)
cultivation, gardening, horticulture, farming, floriculture, husbandry, tillage
The Indian economy depends mainly upon the practice of agriculture.

aim (n.)
aspiration, endeavour, design, goal, mark, inclination, object, end, intent, purpose
My aim is to work in NGOs to help people who are in need.

air (n.)
appearance, demeanour, manner, look, bearing, expression, mien, style, behaviour, fashion
Abraham Lincoln's persona had an air of mystery around him.

airy (adj.)
aerial, ethereal, joyous, lively, fairy-like, gay, light, sprightly, frolicsome
The hotels in Kerala had large and airy rooms.

alarm (n., v.)
affright, disquietude, fright, apprehension, dread, terror, consternation, fear, panic.
Everyone was alarmed due to the sudden black-out in the building. (v.)
He raised an alarm after taking a wig for the face of a demon. (n.)

alert (adj.)
active, lively, prepared, vigilant, brisk, prompt, watchful, ready, wide-awake
The police officer was alert on duty due to the hovering threats of an attack.

alien (adj.)
conflicting, inappropriate, strange, contradictory, foreign, irrelevant, unconnected, contrary,

hostile
The inclusion of the notorious elements in our meet seemed to be an alien approach.

alien (n.)
foreigner, stranger, outsider, interloper
There has been suspicious alien activity in the past few days, which has been reported by the U.S. government.

alike (adj.)
akin, similar, equivalent, same, analogous, homogeneous, like, similar, identical, resembling
Two persons who are friends are alike in some way or the other.

alive (adj.)
active, alert, animate, breathing, live, existent, living
Optimists try to keep the hope alive for themselves and also for the people around them.

allay (v.)
alleviate, appease, compose, quiet, still, soothe, tranquilise, pacify
The baby-sitter allayed the fears of the baby, and put him to sleep in no time.

allege (v.)
adduce, claim, maintain, declare, say, affirm, assert, cite
The bank alleged that my credentials were not up to the mark, and thus the loan would not be sanctioned.

allegiance (n.)
devotion, fealty, faithfulness, loyalty, obedience
This great social worker's long allegiance to public service is noteworthy.

allegory (n.)
apologue, exemplum, fable, fiction, illustration, metaphor, parable
An allegory is essentially a short moral tale with animals as its central characters.
It is easier to explain things to children with the help of allegorical stories.

alleviate (v.)
abate, lighten, reduce, remove, assuage, mitigate, relieve, lessen

This palliative would alleviate your body ache.

alliance (n.)

bond, coalition, fusion, partnership, confederation, federation, union

The final writing down of the will is not possible because of the shifting alliances within a large family.

allot (v.)

appoint, give, portion out, apportion, distribute, grant, select, assign, divide, set apart

The school kids were allotted new uniforms for the Independence Day parade.

We had allotted a certain budget to this company for a purpose.

allow (v.)

admit, consent to, let, sanction, tolerate, concede, grant, permit

The teachers decided not to allow the college students to go on a trip without parental approval.

alloy (n.)

admixture, adulteration, debasement, metal

Brass is an alloy of zinc and copper.

allude (v.)

advert, indicate, intimate, point, signify, hint, refer, suggest

She alluded to some issues at her home but didn't clearly mention it.

allure (n. & v.)

attract, captivate, entice, lure, tempt, cajole, coax, draw, seduce

He has the natural allure to tempt anyone. (n.)

She allured him to do what he did not intend to do. (v.)

also (adv.)

as well, in addition, likewise, too, as well as, in like manner, similarly, besides

Shane has a Bentley and he has a Ferrari also.

alternative (n. & adj.)

choice, election, option, pick, preference, resource, substitute

We couldn't have helped him; there was no alternative. (n.)

All the people working there have to come

up with an alternative option. (adj.)

amass (v.)
accumulate, collect, compile, pile up, heap up, hoard up, store up, aggregate, gather, hoard
People in the recent times are focussing on amassing a lot of wealth for absurd reasons.

amateur (n. & adj.)
dilettante, novice, tyro, inexpert, unskilled
Nancy is an amateur in the realm of art. (n.)
He has done a very amateur white-washing job in the house. (adj.)

amaze (v.)
astonish, astound, surprise, bedazzle, bewilder, stupefy, confuse
To be kind-hearted amongst such degradation is something that amazes me.

amazement (n.)
admiration, awe, confusion, surprise, astonishment, bewilderment, perplexity, wonder, stupefaction
She shifted her gaze to him in sheer amazement.
Her capacity to multitask is a matter of amazement.

ambition (n.)
aspiration, competition, emulation, dream
The ambition of every human being is to be successful.

amend (v.)
advance, correct, meliorate, rectify, ameliorate, emend, mend, reform, better, improve, mitigate, repair
It is imperative to amend the manuscript before sending it for publication.

amiable (adj.)
agreeable, engaging, lovable, pleasing, attractive, gentle, cordial, lovely, sweet, benignant, good-natured, loving, genial, charming, kind, pleasant
With all those people present, one can say it was an amiable gathering.

amid (prep.)
amidst, amongst, betwixt, among, between, in the midst of
I looked in every nook

and corner of the house, and I found the dog bone amid the flowers.

amplify (v.)

augment, dilate, expand, extend, unfold, hyperbolise, enlarge, expatiate, increase, exaggerate, blow up

The criminal charges for the alleged robbery were amplified.

I can't hear the music; please amplify the sound.

analogy (n.)

affinity, likeness, relation, similarity, coincidence, resemblance, comparison, similitude

The analogy between a woman and the moon is a cliché.

One can draw an analogy between two similar things.

anger (n. & v.)

fury, rage, choler, ire, wrath, resentment, displeasure, indignation, temper, exasperation, pique

He was overcome by this feeling of anger. (n.)

The horrible performance of the students angered the tutor. (v.)

animal (n. & adj.)

beast, fauna, brute, living creature, living organism, carnal, sensual

We were on a trek and came across a strange animal that came at us out of nowhere. (n.)

Even after so many years of civilisation, human beings are not completely free from their animal instincts. (adj.)

announce (v.)

advertise, proclaim, circulate, give out, promulgate, say, communicate, herald, propound, declare, make known, publish, state, notify, report, declare, annunciate, harbinger

The head of the institution announced the opening of the sports meet.

answer (v. & n.)

rejoinder, repartee, reply, response, retort, tell, state

There are some philosophical questions that cannot be answered. (v.)

I stopped waiting for his answer long back. (n.)

anticipate (v.)
predict, forecast, hope, expect, foretaste, look forward to, prognosticate, forebode
The people could anticipate the selection of Mr. Modi for the post of Prime Minister in India.

anticipation (n.)
expectation, foresight, hope, foreboding, foretaste, presentiment, expectancy, forecast, prevision, prediction
Every member of the family has their own set of anticipations.

antipathy (n.)
disgust, distaste, hatred, repugnance, antagonism, dislike, hostility, repulsion, aversion, detestation
I could never understand her antipathy towards cats.

antique (adj., v. & n.)
ancient, antiquate, age-old, old-timer, quaint, old geezer, gaffer
In Italy, one would come across many antique items in the street. (adj.)
The man standing around the corner is antique. (n.)
All of us were antiquing on the weekend. (v.)

anxiety (n.)
anguish, disquiet, apprehension, disturbance, fretfulness, care, dread, fretting, concern, fear, worry
Charlie's wife is ridden with constant anxiety about his alcohol issues.

apathy (n.)
indifference, insensibility, immobility, unconcern, stillness, unfeelingness, numbness, spiritlessness
The modern-day generation has an unshakeable sense of apathy towards everything.

apiece (adv.)
distributively, each, individually, separately, severally, for each one, to each one
In the kitty, all the women received ₹ 500 apiece.

apology (n.)
acknowledgement, excuse, plea, exculpation, justification, vindication
He wrote a letter of apology to the guest for

the oversight at the night of hosting.

apparent (adj.)
likely, presumable, probable, seeming, plain, evident
His guilt is apparent in every act to all observers.

appear (v.)
have the appearance of, semblance of, look, seem, come out, come along
This equation appeared to be a difficult one, but now it is solved.
Every decade a new star appears in the industry.

appendage (n.)
accessory, appurtenance, accompaniment, adjunct, attachment, extension, auxiliary, supplement, outgrowth
It is imperative that the appendages should be kept covered.

appetite (n.)
appetence, propensity, craving, desire, appetency
It is commendable to see that old man's appetite for life.

apportion (v.)
allot, allocate, distribute, grant, appoint, assign, dispense, divide, share, deal, portion out, divvy
I am going to apportion this chocolate to everyone in an equal manner.

approximation (n.)
approach, likeness, resemblance, estimation, idea, nearness, propinquity
The several mediums of media give only an approximation of the real instances.

arm (n. & v.)
limb, branch, subdivision, accouterments, armour, harness, mail, weapons, blazonry, munition
He has incredibly long arms. (n.)
Every country keeps arms and ammunition to use in times of war for its protection. (n.)
The troops are arming on the border of the rival country. (v.)

army (n.)
armament, forces, military, soldiers, soldiery, force, legions, phalanx, troops
A standing army is employed by every

country to operate in the times of crisis.

arraign (v.)
accuse, charge, impeach, prosecute, indict, summon, incriminate
They were to be arraigned for the deplorable deed they had committed in the past.

array (n. & v.)
collection, arrangement, disposition, order, show, exhibition, sight, raiment, lay out, range
The success of one country over another depends entirely on their array of troops in battle order. (n.)
People are coming over to our house, and, therefore, I want you to array your clothes properly. (v.)

arrest (n. & v.)
detain, restrain, stop, capture, hold, secure, take into custody, catch, make prisoner, seize, take prisoner, halt
This confusion is going to arrest the progress for the project. (v.)
The negotiations are in arrest in the particular scenario. (n.)

artifice (n.)
art, craft, ruse, stratagem, cunning, fraud, machination, guile, trick, wile
She is trained in the art of artifice.

artist (n.)
artificer, artisan, operative, workman, creator
Every artist creates art for an enthusiastic audience.

ask (v.)
entreat, petition, request, solicit, beseech, demand, implore, pray, require, inquire, call for
She always remembers to ask about everyone's health.

associate (v. & n.)
accomplice, comrade, fellow, mate, ally, colleague, friend, partner, companion, helpmate, peer, companion
It is funny how he associates himself with strange people. (v.)
All the associates from his company are coming in for the meeting. (n.)

association (n.)
alliance, familiarity,

lodge, club, federation, participation, community, partnership, connection, fraternity, society, company, corporation
Her association of her mother with being beaten was too strong to break.

assume (v.)
accept, arrogate, postulate, put on, presume, affect, claim, presume, take, appropriate, feign, pretend, take over
I assume his bus was already late.
He acceded to assume the responsibility for the meeting.

assurance (n.)
authority, boldness, self-confidence, confidence, self-reliance, self-assertion, trust, sureness
Her assurance in her superiority did not make her famous.

astute (adj.)
acute, discerning, sharp, clear-sighted, penetrative, shrewd, keen, knowing, sagacious, savvy
An astute businessman always reads the small print in a contract.

attachment (n.)
adherence, devotion, affixation, adhesion, inclination, tenderness, bond
His gesture shows his attachment to his friends.

attack (v.)
beset, combat, invade, assault, besiege, encounter, set upon, beleaguer, charge, fall upon
We were attacked by the enemy with arms and ammunition.

attack (n.)
aggression, incursion, invasion, onslaught, assault, infringement, onset, trespass, encroachment, intrusion
The enemy made an attack upon our side.

attain (v.)
accomplish, gain, master, reach, achieve, get, obtain, secure, acquire, earn, grasp, procure, win, reach
He could attain what he wanted despite all the setbacks that came his way.

attitude (n.)
pose, position, posture, orientation, mannerism
The actor struck just the right attitude for the role.

attribute (v.)
ascribe, associate, connect, impute, refer, assign
It is uncharitable to attribute evil motives to others.

attribute (n.)
property, quality, characteristic, dimension, trait, feature
Divinity is an attribute of God.

augur (n. & v.)
auspex (n.), auspicate, foreshadow, betoken, divine, foretell, predict, prognosticate, bode, forebode, portend, presage, prophesy
We augur from all events a prosperous result. (v.)
He is an augur who could take such a huge responsibility. (n.)

authentic (adj.)
accepted, bona fide, certain, original, sure, accredited, real, true, authoritative, genuine, trustworthy, authorised, legitimate, reliable, veritable
We have cross-checked from his accounts; this is an authentic signature.

auxiliary (n. & v.)
accessory, ally, appurtenant, adjunct, adjuvant, coadjutor, helper, promoter, aid, assistant, confederate, mercenary, subordinate (n.)
subsidiary, supplemental, supplementary (adj.)
Everyone wants to be an auxiliary in a good cause. (n.)
The main library and its auxiliary branches can be seen in the model. (adj.)

avaricious (adj.)
greedy, grasping, prehensile, niggardly, penurious, sordid, covetous, rapacious
He was a great monarch, but the flaw in his character was that he was avaricious.

avenge (v.)
punish, retaliate, revenge, vindicate, visit
His brother was

murdered and, therefore, he wants to avenge the wrong-doing committed against his brother.

avow (v.)

aver, assert, affirm, own, profess, testify, admit, avouch, declare, proclaim, swear, verify

An innocent person does not fear to avow in front of the Almighty.

awful (adj.)

abominable, alarming, direful, frightful, appalling, dreadful, horrible, portentous, terrible, fearful, shocking

We could overhear the awful voices outside the room, where the crime took place.

It is rather awful that all of us could not stay together for long.

awkward (adj.)

boorish, rough, unhandy, bungling, gawky, uncouth, clownish, maladroit, ungainly, uneasy

The new recruit is awkward at the business of making food.

It was quite an awkward situation with the strangers in the room.

axiom (n.)

aphorism, truism, maxim, proposition

The doctrine of the divine right originated with the axiom that the king can do no wrong.

Several axioms have been created for the moral health of the society.

□

babble (v. & n.)

blab, cackle, gabble, murmur, prattle, blurt, chat, gossip, palaver, tattle, blurt out, chatter, jabber, prate, twaddle

It is not uncommon to see the sick man babbling of home. (v.)

The babble of a baby is a source of happiness. (n.)

banish (v.)

ban, dismiss, evict, expatriate, ostracise, discharge, drive out, exile, expel, oust, dislodge, eject

Salman Rushdie was banished from India for his book *The Satanic Verses*.

bank (n. & v.)

beach, bound, brink, edge, margin, shore, border, brim, coast, marge, rim, strand, trust (n.)

transact, shut in, tip, give, believe (v.)

We have deposited some money in the bank to keep it safe. (n.)

They sat on the bank of the river and enjoyed what nature had to offer. (n.)

She banks her pay-cheque every month. (v.)

One should bank on one's good education for crisis in their lives. (v.)

banter (n. & v.)

jeering, raillery, sarcasm, chaff, kid, josh, jolly, irony, mockery, ridicule, satire, repartee

We like to have some senseless banter when we are with friends. (n.)

She keeps on bantering with Sophie until she is frustrated. (v.)

barbarous (adj.)

atrocious, brutal, merciless, uncivilised, barbarian, cruel, rude, uncouth, barbaric, inhuman, savage, inhumane

It was undoubtedly one of the most barbarous crimes that I have seen till date.

barrier (n.)
bar, bulwark, block, obstruction, rampart, barricade, hindrance, restraint, obstacle, prohibition, restriction
There are numerous barriers to progress in this country.

battle (n. & v.)
action, combat, encounter, passage of arms, affair, conflict, engagement (n.)
struggle, bout, contest, fight (v.)
He fought the battle for the purpose of achieving martyrdom. (n.)
She has been battling cancer for the last two years. (v.)

beat (v. & n.)
chastise, overcome, thrash, batter, strike, vanquish, belabor, pound, surpass, whip, bruise, defeat, scourge, flog (v.)
sound, routine (n.)
She had to beat him up with a stick over his head to get him to his sense. (v.)
The beat of the music was too gripping. (n.)
Every policeman had to walk a beat and knew all his people by name. (n.)

beautiful (adj.)
attractive, charming, exquisite, handsome, beauteous, comely, fair, lovely, bewitching, delightful, fine, picturesque, elegant, graceful, pretty
This particular picture appears beautiful to the eye.

because (conj.)
as, for, inasmuch as, since
I couldn't reach my place because I had missed my train.

becoming (adj. & v.)
befitting, congruous, fit, meet, seemly, beseeming, decent, fitting, neat, suitable, comely, decorous, graceful, proper, worthy
The outfit was becoming to the one wearing it. (v.)
Such behaviour was becoming in her. (adj.)

beginning (n., v. & adj.)
arising, inauguration,

commencement, inception, outset, spring, fount, initiation, rise, start, fountain, opening (n.)
first, seminal, origin, source (adj.)
commencing, setting out, starting (v.)
He knew it from the very beginning that she was the girl for him. (n.)
The beginning section of this poem seems to be difficult. (adj.)
A terrible murder begins in the book and then there is no turning back. (v.)

behaviour (n.)
action, conduct, deportment, manner, bearing, demeanour, life, manners
The behaviour of the clergyman towards his people was not appreciated.

bend (n. & v.)
bias, diverge, mould, submit, bow, deflect, incline, persuade, turn, warp, deviate, influence, stoop, twine, yield (v.)
curve, crook, twist, turn (n.)
The plastic stick does not bend, even if you try too hard. (v.)
There is a bend in the road a little further ahead. (n.)

benevolence (n.)
alms-giving, charity, kind-heartedness, munificence, beneficence, benefaction, generosity, kindliness, philanthropy, benignity, kindness, bounty
The benevolence of the wealthy towards the poor is a common sight these days.

bind (v. & n.)
attach, compel, fetter, oblige, restrict, shackle, engage, fix, restrain, secure, tie, fasten
The dictator is known to bind one in chains to torture them endlessly. (v.)
It is a bind that would hinder the breaching of contract. (n.)

bitter (adj., n. & adv.)
acerbic, acidulous, caustic, pungent, stinging, acetous, acrid, cutting, acid, acrimonious, harsh, sharp, biting, irate

The bitter truth is that everyone is selfish. (adj.)
The dish tastes bitter. (n.)
It seems to be bitter cold outside. (adv.)

bleach (n. & v.)
blanch, make white, whiten, whitewash (v.)
whitener, bleaching agent, blanching agent (n.)
Complete bleach usually requires several applications. (n.)
I have asked the maid to bleach the laundry. (v.)

blemish (n. & v.)
blot, deface, disgrace, injury, spot, defect, dishonour, reproach, stain, deformity, fault, smirch, stigma, dent, flaw, soil, taint, daub, disfigurement, tarnish
It is a blemish on the character of a society when a woman is molested. (n.)
Her face was blemished because of the trauma caused to her. (v.)

blow (n. & v.)
box, concussion, disaster, misfortune, knock, rap, stroke, calamity, cut, lash, shock (n.)
drift, afloat, botch up, muck up, spoil (v.)
It was a big blow for him to see his house charred in fire. (n.)
The leaves were blowing in the breeze. (v.)
She blew up the party when she fell. (v.)

bluff (n., adj. & v.)
impolite, rough, blunt, coarse, inconsiderate, rude, blustering, discourteous, open, uncivil, bold, frank, plain-spoken, unmannerly (adj.)
lie, fake, pretend, dissimulate (n. & v.)
His bluff succeeded in getting him accepted. (n.)
He bluffed about his strengths. (v.)
She has a bluff but unpleasant manner. (adj.)

body (n.)
torso, frame, system, carcass, corpse, form, trunk, anatomy, cadaver
She felt as if her whole body was on fire.

both (pro. & adj. & conj.)
twain, two
She would like both skirts. (pro.)
Both men look

handsome. (adj.)
She is both kind and considerate. (conj.)

boundary (n.)
barrier, confines, limit, margin, border, edge, line, term, frontier, marge, verge
The boundaries of an estate are set to keep the intruders at bay.
The boundary between neighbouring territories is imperative for defining the space of these nations.

brave (adj., v. & n.)
adventurous, courageous, fearless, undaunted, bold, daring, gallant, dauntless, heroic, valiant, intrepid, venturesome, unfearing
Facing deadly and fatal situations and coming out unhurt makes a brave person braver. (adj.)
The world became a place that it is because of the explorers who braved the difficulties. (v.)
The army is a space of the brave. (n.)

break (v. & n.)
crack, destroy, shatter, split, burst, crush, fracture, rupture, shiver, demolish, rend, sever, smash, transgress, terminate
People are known to break and make laws according to their convenience. (v.)
A glass can break into several pieces. (v.)
There was a break in the action when the actor was hurt in the shoot. (n.)

brutish (adj.)
animal, brutal, ignorant, sensual, base, unintellectual, beastly, carnal, bestial
He is a brutish and a dull person.

burn (v. & n.)
blaze, char, flame, incinerate, consume, flash, kindle, set on fire, cauterise, cremate, ignite, scorch
She accidentally burned down the house. (v.)
He had a sunburn during his vacation. (n.)

business (n.)
affair, commerce, handicraft, trade, concern, job, occupation, transaction, barter, duty, employment, work

He is going to inherit the business of his father.

but (conj. & adv.)
however, notwithstanding, just, only, merely, provided, unless, except, moreover, save, yet, further, nevertheless, still
She went to bed but could not sleep. (conj.)
There is hope that lasts but a moment. (adv.)

by (prep. & adv.)
through, with, near, past
His house which was going to be destroyed by the terrorists was saved by the government. (prep.)
It is every hour a bus goes by. (adv.)

□

C

cabal (n. & v.)
machination, confederacy, crew, gang, complot, conspiracy, faction, junto, plot
It is clearly a cabal against the present government; so, the officials have to be careful. (n.)
He has successfully caballed what was needed. (v.)

calculate (v.)
account, consider, enumerate, rate, cast, count, estimate, reckon, compute, deem, number, sum up
It is vain to calculate upon an uncertain result.

call (v. & n.)
roar, shriek, bellow, ejaculate, scream, vociferate, clamour, exclaim, shout, yell (v.)
cry, phone call, shout (n.)
They called his daughter to see him in his final times. (v.)
There was an important phone call for the president in the morning. (n.)

calm (adj., v. & n.)
collected, imperturbable, sedate, still, composed, peaceful, self-possessed, tranquil, cool, placid, serene, undisturbed, dispassionate, quiet, smooth, unruffled
She spoke to him in a calm voice. (adj.)
You need to calm yourself to think clearly. (v.)
There was calm all around. (n.)

cancel (v.)
nullify, rescind, abrogate, revoke, annul, erase, quash, rub off or out, blot out, expunge, remove, scratch out, cross off or out
She picked up the phone instantly and cancelled the dinner party.

candid (adj.)
honest, open, truthful, artless, simple, sincere, frank, innocent, straightforward, unreserved, guileless
One has to be candid with a friend and not a foe.

caparison (n. & v.)
accouterments, barde (v.)
harness, housings, trappings (n.)
He wore a caparison for the show. (n.)
For the occasion, they had to caparison the horses. (v.)

capital (n. & adj.)
chief city, metropolis, seat of government, centre (n.)
primary, important, great, majuscule (adj.)
The capital is power source in the political sense.
Our capital concern is to protect our citizens. (adj.)

care (v. & n.)
anxiety, concern, attention, vigilance, caution, forethought, precaution, wariness, heed, prudence, watchfulness, circumspection, worry
One needs to take care for the future. (n.)
She cared for him during his illness. (v.)

career (v. & n.)
charge, flight, passage, race, rush (v.)
course, calling, public life, vocation (n.)
As a career option, I am seriously considering Lectureship. (n.)
The buses careered down the street. (v.)

caress (n. & v.)
coddle, embrace, fondle, pamper, court, flatter, kiss, pet
He caressed her face with his hand; caressed by admirers. (v.)
She showered him with caresses. (n.)

caricature (n. & v.)
burlesque, extravaganza, mimicry, take-off, exaggeration, imitation, parody, travesty
The cartoon caricatured the Prime Minister. (v.)
It is a caricature of the President. (n.)

carry (v.)
bear, convey, move, sustain, transmit, bring, lift, remove, take,

transport, contain
It was his job to carry the furniture to the new house.

catastrophe (n.)
calamity, denouement, mischance, mishap, cataclysm, disaster, misfortune, sequel
The catastrophe in his life seemed almost impossible to recover from.

catch (v. & n.)
comprehend, grasp, overtake, snatch, capture, grip, secure, take, clasp, ensnare, gripe, seize, take hold of, clutch, entrap
We have to catch this fugitive by the collar. (v.)
Our catch was only 15 crabs after spending six hours in the ocean. (n.)

cause (n. & v.)
causality, occasion, precedent, agent, former, origin, reason, antecedent, condition, fountain, origin, source, author, creator
The cause of the disaster was clear from the very beginning itself. (n.)
The disaster was caused by him. (v.)

cease (v.)
abstain, desist, give over, quit, bring to an end, discontinue, refrain, end, stop, conclude, finish, pause
She should cease teasing her little brother.

celebrate (v.)
commemorate, keep, observe, solemnise, mark, felicitate
We celebrate the day with the required ceremonies.

center (n. & v.)
middle, midst (n.)
focus on, concentrate on, revolve about, revolve around (v.)
This restaurant is in the center of town. (n.)
Her attention was always centered on her husband. (v.)

chagrin (n. & v.)
confusion, humiliation, shame, disappointment, dismay, mortification, vexation
She felt deep chagrin at on account of failure. (n)
He chagrined his colleague in front of the head of the department.

change (v.)
alter, exchange, shift, transmute, metamorphose, substitute, turn, convert, modify, transfigure, vary, transform
It is a fascinating process to witness the change from a caterpillar into a butterfly.

change (n.)
alteration, mutation, transmutation, conversion, novelty, revolution, variation, diversity, transformation, variety, innovation, transition
The country has made a change for the better.
The change of a liquid into a gas is basically called evaporation.

character (n.)
constitution, genius, personality, temper, disposition, nature, record, spirit, temperament
The character of the applicant is above suspicion.

characteristic (n. & adj.)
attribute, feature, peculiarity, sign, character, indication, property, trait, mark, quality
Humility is one of her best characteristics. (n.)
She saw her friend's characteristic smirk. (adj.)

charming (adj.)
bewitching, delightful, enrapturing, fascinating, captivating, enchanting, entrancing
She narrated those charming incantations to cast a spell upon him.

chasten (v.)
chastise, discipline, punish, subdue, castigate, correct, purify, tame, rebuke
He chastened him for his inappropriate statements.

cherish (v.)
care for, harbour, nurse, cling to, entertain, hold dear, nurture, treasure, foster, nourish, protect, value
They should cherish their hard-earned freedom.

choose (v.)
cull, elect, opt, pick, pick out, prefer, select, take
It is difficult to choose a

good husband for your daughter.

circumlocution (n.)
diffuseness, prolixity, verbiage, periphrasis, verbosity, pleonasm, wordiness
The question-and-answer round with the minister was just an act of circumlocution on his part.

circumstance (n.)
accompaniment, fact, point, occurrence, position, detail, incident, particular, situation
We can also think of another circumstance and the time it would take.

class (n. & v.)
circle, company, grade, rank, caste, clan, club, coterie, order, set, category, family
Everyone is sleeping in the morning classes. (n.)
Al Pacino has shown a lot of class in *The Godfather*. (n.)
How would you class these ancient coins – historic or prehistoric?

cleanse (v.)
brush, dust, purify, scour, sponge, wash, clean, lave, wipe, disinfect
The hall was cleansed by the servants with soap and water.

clear (adj., v., n. & adv.)
apparent, intelligible, pellucid, transparent, perspicuous, unadorned, distinct, lucid, plain, unambiguous, evident, manifest, straightforward, unequivocal, explicit, obvious
To solve a complex problem, one requires a clear head. (adj.)
We should clear the path through this dense forest to make things easy. (v.)
She cried loud and clear. (adv.)
The investigation revealed that she was in the clear. (n.)

clever (adj.)
sharp, adroit, dexterous, ingenious, knowing, skilful, apt, quick, smart, intelligent, quick-witted
It is a clever tool to be used.

collision (n.)
clash, contact, hit, impact,

opposition, clashing, conflict, encounter
The collision of two trucks coming from the opposite directions led to the accident.

comfortable (adj.)
snug, at ease, well-off, at rest, contented, well-provided, satisfied, well-to-do, comfy
She felt comfortable at her parents' house.

commit (v.)
assign, consign, entrust, relegate, devote, give, invest
She committed a heinous crime in a fit of passion.

company (n.)
assemblage, assembly, crowd, meeting, congregation, gathering, convention, group, throng
The company of chefs walked into the restaurant to receive thanks for an amazing menu.

compel (v.)
coerce, drive, make, constrain, force, necessitate, oblige, obligate
We have to compel her to sit for the exam.

complain (v.)
croak, growl, grunt, remonstrate, find fault, grumble, murmur, repine
The lawyer had to complain that the defendant had abused his client.

complex (adj. & n.)
abstruse, confused, intricate, mixed, complicated, composite, entangled, manifold, compound, heterogeneous, mingled, tangled
It seems to be a complex set of variations based on a simple folk music. (adj.)
It is the complex of shopping malls, houses, and roads that leads to the creation of a new city. (n.)

condemn (v.)
blame, convict, reprove, censure, objurgate, reprobate, sentence
The murderer was condemned to death for her heinous crime.

confess (v.)
accept, allow, concede, grant, acknowledge, avow, disclose, own, admit, recognise
He confessed that he had committed the murder.

confirm (v.)
assure, fix, sanction, substantiate, corroborate, prove, settle, sustain, establish, uphold
One can easily confirm the statements by looking at the testimony.
It needs persistence to confirm a person in a belief.

congratulate (v.)
compliment, felicitate
She congratulated him upon his success in the company for remarkable work.

conquer (v.)
beat, overthrow, subject, checkmate, master, prevail over, subjugate, crush, overcome, put down, surmount, defeat, overmaster, reduce, vanquish, win, down, overpower, subdue
You cannot have everything you desire always; you need to conquer your desires.

conscious (adj.)
assured, certain, cognizant, sensible, apprised, aware, certified, informed, sure, deliberate
In the poem *The Ancient Mariner*, one witnesses that on the stormy sea, a man is conscious of the limitation of human power.

consequence (n.)
end, issue, effect, event, outcome, result, aftermath, upshot, ramification, repercussion, outcome
If we do not control our use of polluting substances, then it could have grave consequences for planet Earth.

console (v. & n.)
comfort, condole with, encourage, sympathise with, solace, soothe
He for his passion in music-mixing bought a DJ console. (n.)
We had to console her for the untimely death of her father. (v.)

contagion (n.)
infection, transmission
The whole place is in a state of contagion.

It was a contagion of mirth all around.

continual (adj.)
ceaseless, incessant, regular, uninterrupted, constant, invariable, unbroken, unremitting, continuous, perpetual, unceasing, persistent, repeated
There was a continual banging of the doors by the patient to be heard by the doctor.

contract (n. & v.)
agreement, cartel, engagement, pledge, arrangement, compact, obligation, pact, shrink, undertake
The companies had to sign a contract to resolve the issues. (n.)
The heat contracted the woolen clothes. (v.)
He contracted a chill when he went for a trip to the mountains. (v.)

contrast (n. & v.)
compare, differentiate, discriminate, oppose, counterpoint, demarcate
To know how the products are different, we contrast one product with another. (v.)
The contrast in the television is too high; it could hurt children's eyes. (n.)

conversation (n.)
chat, communion, converse, dialogue, communication, conference, discourse, talk
The conversation with friends should lighten up his mood.

convert (v. & n.)
disciple, neophyte, proselyte (n.)
change, transform, alter, exchange (v.)
He is a convert; he was uncomfortable with his old religious faith. (n.)
The Christians had to convert many people to popularise their religious faith. (v.)

convey (v.)
carry, give, remove, shift, transmit, express, bring, get, take
Please convey my message to your friend when you meet her.
We had to convey from the house to the station.

convoke (v.)
assemble, call together, convene, collect, gather,

summon
The politicians were convoked in the meeting hall.

criminal (n. & adj.)
abominable, immoral, sinful, vile, culpable, guilty, iniquitous, unlawful, wicked, illegal, nefarious, vicious (adj.)
felon, outlaw, crook, malefactor (n.)
He is a criminal in the eyes of law. (n.)
What he has done is a criminal offence, and there is no excuse for it. (v.)

□

daily (adv., adj. & n.)
diurnal, everyday, day after day
She stops by daily to check on the children. (adv.)
We saw the news in that daily. (n.)
These are my daily clothes and slippers. (adj.)

danger (n.)
hazard, jeopardy, peril, risk, menace, threat
This step can pose as a great danger to your plans for the future.

dark (adj. & n.)
black, dusky, gloomy, obscure, shadowy, murky, shady, swarthy
She moved towards the dark without realising the dangers that lie ahead for her. (n.)
I could see him sitting in a dark corner, guilty of what he had done. (adj.)

decay (n. & v.)
corrupt, decompose, molder, putrefy, rot, spoil, decomposition, crumble, disintegrate
The house is in such a state of decay that it is impossible to rebuild it. (n.)
The corpse of her mother had started to decay and needed to be cremated. (v.)

deception (n.)
craft, dissimulation, lie, cunning, double-dealing, fraud, lying, deceit, duplicity, guile, prevarication, deceitfulness, fabrication, hypocrisy, trickery, delusion, falsehood
He is a master of deception; there is no contending this fact.

defense (n.)
apology, guard, shelter, bulwark, justification, resistance, shield, fortress, protection, safeguard, vindication
One has to up one's defense against assault.

defile (n. & v.)
befoul, corrupt, pollute, spoil, sully, tarnish, contaminate, soil, stain, taint desecrate, taint
The temple was defiled by sacrilegious deeds of the atheists. (v.)
We had to pass that defile to cross-over. (n.)

definition (n.)
comment, description, exposition, rendering, commentary, explanation, interpretation, translation
The thorough work-out had given her body a great definition.
We need to get acquainted with the definition of this word before using it in a sentence.

delegate (v. & n.)
deputy, legate, proxy, representative, substitute (n.)
assign, depute, designate (v.)
I have delegated all the responsibilities to all the members of the team for efficient working of the company. (v.)
He is a delegate from the United States of America, who had come in for the conference. (n.)

deliberate (adj. & v.)
confer, consult, meditate, reflect, consider, debate, ponder, weigh
We deliberate upon the concerning a matter and come to a conclusion. (v.)
He has done deliberate damage to harm the company. (adj.)

delicious (adj.)
dainty, delightful, exquisite, luscious, savory, scrumptious, yummy, delectable
The food at that Chinese restaurant is delicious; you should try it sometime.

delightful (adj.)
delicious, pleasant, refreshing, agreeable, grateful, pleasing, satisfying, congenial, gratifying, pleasurable
It was such a delightful surprise to see him after so many years.

delusion (n.)
error, fallacy, hallucination, illusion, phantasm
She has delusions about her beauty, which stand to be corrected.

demolish (v.)
destroy, overthrow, overturn, raze, ruin, pulverise, crush, smash
In the event of war, both sides want to demolish the other.

demonstration (n.)
certainty, evidence, inference, conclusion, deduction, induction, proof, presentation, monstrance
She gave the customer a demonstration of the product that he was interested in.

design (v. & n.)
aim, final cause, object, proposal, device, intent, plan, purpose, end, intention, project, scheme
His design of defrauding was a masterful one which no one could detect. (n.)
We had to design the costumes ourselves for the fashion show. (v.)

desire (n. & v.)
appetite, coveting, inclination, propensity, aspiration, craving, longing, wish, want
His is the desire for fame and excellence. (n.)
I desire to achieve the best for everyone in the institution. (v.)

despair (n. & v.)
desperation, despondency, discouragement, hopelessness
One should not despair even in hard times. (v.)
She is too sensitive, so much so that one harsh word would send her into the depths of despair. (n.)

dexterity (n.)
adroitness, aptitude, cleverness, expertness, readiness, skill, sleight
One needs dexterity of hand to do minute work, such as embroidery or jewellery designing.

diction (n.)
expression, phrase, style, vocabulary, language, phraseology, verbiage, wording, phrasing, wordage
The diction of this document sounds too pedantic.

die (v. & n.)
cease, decline, expire, perish, decease, depart, fade, wither

He died by violence, fighting for his country. (v.)
In Mahabharata's Dicing game, the die played an instrumental role. (n.)

difference (n.)
contrariety, discrimination, distinction, inequality, contrast, disparity, unlikeness, dissimilarity, diversity, variation, discrepancy, dissimilitude, inconsistency
There is always a difference between the old and the new generation and their ideas.

difficult (adj.)
arduous, hard, onerous, toilsome, exhausting, laborious, unmanageable
These are indeed difficult times.

direction (n.)
aim, bearing, course, inclination, tendency, way, guidance, focus
When the family needed help, the son looked in the other direction.
A new council was installed under the direction of the king.

discern (v.)
discriminate, observe, recognise, distinguish, perceive, see, make out, understand
She is smart enough to discern the situation.

discover (v.)
ascertain, detect, disclose, ferret out, find out, expose, find, invent, come upon
She discovered high levels of lead in her drinking water.
We need to discover the evidence to prove the crime.

disease (n.)
disorder, sickness, ailment, distemper, infirmity, unhealthiness, illness, malady, unsoundness
Cancer is a deadly disease; however, the doctors across the world are struggling to find a cure for that.

disparage (v.)
belittle, depreciate, discredit, underestimate, derogate from, dishonour, under-rate, lower, undervalue
The critics have

disparaged the author's vision in their critical review.

displace (v.)
confuse, disturb, mislay, remove, disarrange, jumble, misplace, unsettle, move
The war displaces many people every time it happens.

do (n. & v.)
accomplish, carry out, perform, achieve, carry through, perpetrate, actualise, commit, execute, realise, complete, finish, transact, bring to pass, fulfill
One has to do research for the term papers. (v.)
There is an elite do (party) in the hall downstairs. (n.)

docile (adj.)
amenable, manageable, pliant, teachable, compliant, obedient, submissive, gentle, tame, yielding
Teachers are eager to teach and tutor docile students.

doctrine (n.)
article of belief, belief, precept, teaching, philosophy, dogma, principle, tenet
The doctrine of sovereign immunity originated with the maxim that the king can do no wrong.

dogmatic (adj.)
arrogant, doctrinal, positive, authoritative, domineering, opinionated, dictatorial, imperious, overbearing, systematic, narrow-minded
Some ancient writings can be dogmatic in their outlook.

doubt (v.)
distrust, mistrust, surmise, suspect, question
To doubt is to lack conviction.

doubt (n.)
disbelief, perplexity, suspense, distrust, indecision, question, suspicion, hesitancy, irresolution, scruple, hesitation, misgiving, skepticism, uncertainty
I doubt that she will accept his proposal of marriage so soon.

draw (v. & n.)
allure, drag, haul, induce,

lure, tow, attract, entice, incline, lead, pull, tug
We need to draw water out of the well. (v.)
The game was inconclusive and ended in a draw. (n.)

dream (n. & v.)
day-dream, fantasy, reverie, trance, fancy, hallucination, romance, vision, aspiration, ambition
She lives in a dream that is far from reality. (n.)
He claims to never dream about anything. (v.)

dress (v., n. & adj.)
apparel, clothes, garb, uniform, array, clothing, garments, raiment, vestments, attire, costume, robes, vesture
All of us had to dress as quickly as possible for the meeting. (v.)
The warriors had to get ready in their battle-dress. (n.)
It was a full-dress ceremony where everyone was invited. (adj.)

drive (v. & n.)
compel, propel, repel, resist, thrust, impel, push, repulse, ride, urge on, cause, ride
We have to drive to market to get the material for the restaurant. (v.)
The team was ready for a drive towards the pennant. (n.)

duplicate (v., n. & adj.)
copy, facsimile, likeness, reproduction, counterpart, imitation, replica, transcript, repeat, double
The polished surface duplicated his body in reverse. (v.)
He always carried duplicates in case of an emergency. (n.)
I also want a duplicate key to the house. (adj.)

duty (n.)
accountability, function, office, right, business, obligation, responsibility, righteousness
It is the duty of every citizen to use resources responsibly.

□

eager (adj.)
animated, desirous, glowing, longing, anxious, earnest, hot, intense, vehement, ardent, enthusiastic, impatient, intent, yearning, burning, fervent, impetuous, keen, zealous
People are eager to fight for the honour of their country. (adj.)

ease (v. & n.)
easiness, expertness, facility, knack, readiness, relief, rest
One could ease the process by sharing one's pain. (v.)
I would prefer a life of luxury and ease over deprivation and discomfort. (n.)

education (n.)
discipline, learning, study, pedagogy, instruction
Shakespeare did not receive any formal education; still, he wrote stellar plays.

effrontery (n.)
boldness, hardihood, insolence, audacity, brass, impudence, shamelessness, presumptuousness
She hated him for his effrontery in the matters of the office.

egotism (n.)
conceit, self-assertion, self-confidence, self-esteem, egoism, self-conceit, self-consciousness, vanity, self-importance
Mr. Darcy was rejected by Elizabeth due to the egotism in his character.

emblem (n.)
attribute, figure, image, sign, symbol, token, type, allegory, symbol
The red colour of rose is an emblem of passion.

emigrate (v.)
immigrate, migrate,

transmigrate
A person emigrates from the land he leaves, and immigrates to the land where he takes up his abode.

employ (v. & n.)
call, engage, engross, hire, make use of, use, use up, utilise
The company is employing him in upon a work for a purpose and at a stipulated salary. (v.)
He was an employ of the city's government. (n.)

end (v.)
break off, close, conclude, expire, quit, terminate, cease, complete, desist, finish, stop, wind up
We have to end this charade of happiness.

end (n.)
accomplishment, effect, limit, achievement, outcome, bound, extent, period, boundary, extremity, point, finale, purpose, close, result, completion, finish, termination, conclusion, consequence, goal, tip, intent, utmost, design
To what end are we doing this pretense of being happy?

endeavour (v.)
attempt, essay, strive, try, undertake, drop, effort, pass by
We endeavour to make people satisfied with our services.

endeavour (n.)
attempt, effort, essay, exertion, struggle, trial, enterprise
I had serious doubts about his endeavours.

endure (v.)
abide, bear, submit to, sustain, afford, bear up, under, permit, suffer, tolerate, allow, bear with
The new generation has to endure a lot of narrow-minded thinking of the previous generation.

enemy (n.)
adversary, competitor, foe, opponent, rival
He was the enemy of my friend in the contest.

enmity (n.)
bitterness, ill-will, malignity, animosity, hatred, malevolence, rancor, antagonism,

hostility, malice, spite
There is blatant enmity between two factions during war.

entertain (v.)
amuse, cheer, disport, enliven, interest, please, beguile, delight, divert, gratify, hold
One should not entertain false notions about the future.
The TV shows nowadays try hard to entertain their audience.

entertainment (n.)
amusement, diversion, fun, pleasure, cheer, enjoyment, merriment, recreation, delight, frolic
We called over the clowns for the sake of entertainment of the kids.

enthusiasm (n.)
ardor, excitement, frenzy, devotion, inspiration, vehemence, eagerness, fanaticism, intensity, warmth, earnestness, fervency, passion, zeal, ecstasy, fervor, ebullience, exuberance
I cannot believe her enthusiasm for dance.

entrance (n. & v.)
access, approach, gate, introduction, accession, door, gateway, opening, adit, doorway, ingress, penetration, admission, inlet, portal, admittance, entry
This gate signals to the entrance into that magical place. (n.)
He entranced all girls' hearts. (v.)

envious (adj.)
jealous, suspicious, covetous
She was envious of her wealth and beauty.

equivocal (adj.)
ambiguous, ambivalent, indistinct, questionable, doubtful, indefinite, obscure, suspicious, dubious, indeterminate, perplexing, uncertain
Philosophers, writers, and artists of all sorts have a peculiar habit of making equivocal statements.

esteem (v.)
appreciate, consider, estimate, prize, think, calculate, deem, hold, regard, value

He esteems himself as a remarkable writer.

esteem (n.)
estimate, estimation, favour, regard, respect
I have lost all esteem for her after witnessing that horrible incident.

eternal (adj.)
fadeless, undying, endless, immortal, unending, aeonian, imperishable, perpetual, unfading, everlasting, interminable, timeless, unfailing, ever-living, never-ending, unceasing
The wait for God to many people proved eternal.

event (n.)
case, contingency, fortune, outcome, chance, end, incident, possibility, circumstance, episode, issue, result, consequence, fact, occurrence
In the case of that event, we would rule out the first possibility.

every (adj.)
all, any, both, each, either
For every correct answer, you would be given a chocolate.

evident (adj.)
apparent, glaring, overt, tangible, clear, indubitable, palpable, transparent, conspicuous, manifest, patent, unmistakable, discernible, obvious, perceptible, visible, distinct, plain
It is clearly evident in the manuscript that it has been altered.

example (n.)
archetype, prototype, type, ensample, model, sample, exemplar, pattern, specimen, precedent
I have to cite an example to support my argument.

excess (adj. & n.)
dissipation, surplus, exorbitance, overplus, redundancy, waste, extravagance, prodigality, superabundance, wastefulness, intemperance, profusion
The woman was spoiled by excess. (n.)
I am trying to shed the excess weight that I have accumulated in the last few months. (adj.)

execute (v.)

administer, carry out, do, enforce, perform, accomplish

We have to execute the decisions of the people as soon as possible.

exercise (n. & v.)

act, application, exertion, performance, action, drill, occupation, activity, employment, operation, use, usage

Let's exercise our exclusive powers over this session. (v.)

The doctor has recommended the patient to exercise regularly. (n.)

expense (n.)

cost, expenditure, disbursal

The business can only flourish if one keeps tab on the expenses done.

explicit (adj.)

express, denotative

The movie had explicit sexual content that could have been easily removed.

extemporaneous (adj.)

extemporary, impromptu, off-hand, extempore, improvised, unpremeditated, unrehearsed, ad-lib

His was an extemporaneous poem recital.

exterminate (v.)

annihilate, eradicate, overthrow, uproot, banish, expel, remove, wipe out, destroy, extirpate, root out

We have exterminate anti-social elements from our society to make it better.

□

faint (adj., v. & n.)
dim, fatigued, irresolute, weak, exhausted, feeble, languid, faded, listless, worn, faint-hearted, ill-defined, purposeless, worn down, faltering, indistinct
I am trying to remember about the past, but it is nothing more than a faint recollection. (adj.)
She fainted after seeing the debacle. (v.)
It was just a spell of faint that came over him after what he saw. (n.)

faith (n.)
confidence, opinion, assurance, conviction, creed, reliance, belief, credence, doctrine, trust
In times of need and otherwise too, you need to have faith in God.

faithful (adj.)
devoted, incorruptible, stanch, true, trusty, firm, loyal, sure, trustworthy, unwavering, constant, true-hearted
We need faithful patriots on duty for commandeering the army.

fame (n.)
eminence, honour, reputation, credit, glory, laurels, renown, repute, distinction, renown
Many people have made it into the Hall of Fame in Madame Tussaud's in London.

fanaticism (n.)
bigotry, credulity, intolerance, superstition, zealotry, fanatism
Sometimes, it so happens that patriotism turns into fanaticism.

fanciful (adj.)
chimerical, fantastic, grotesque, imaginative, visionary, imaginary, notional, illusionary, creative, unreal

She always had a fanciful mind, which did not consider reality at all.

fancy (v. & adj.)
desire, imagination, caprice, inclination, supposition, conceit, idea, liking, vagary, conception, image, mood, whim, fantasy
He obviously fancies her for her beauty. (v.)
She has taken a fancy for him, as he is some handsome and rich. (adj.)

farewell (n. & int.)
adieu, good-bye, parting salutation, valedictory, congé, leave-taking, valediction, send-off
I bade farewell to my comrades. (n.)
We all stopped to say farewell before her flight left. (int.)

fear (n. & v.)
affright, dismay, horror, timidity, apprehension, misgiving, trembling, awe, dread, panic, fright, terror, trepidation
The fear of a divine entity has kept people civilised for so many years. (n.)
I fear I won't be able to make it to your function. (v.)

feminine (adj. & n.)
effeminate, female, womanish, womanly, maidenly, matronly, woman-like
She has feminine virtues of gentleness and compassion. (adj.)
The dress that she was wearing was feminine. (n.)

fetter (n. & v.)
bondage, custody, irons, bonds, handcuffs, manacles, chains, duress, imprisonment, shackles, hobble
When we went to visit him in jail, he was in fetters. (n.)
The old notions fetter our mind, and don't let go forward to new thinking. (v.)

feud (n. & v.)
brawl, dissension, hostility, animosity, broil, controversy, enmity, quarrel, bitterness, contention, dispute
Some epic wars are no more than petty feuds. (n.)
The two friends have

been feuding for years now. (v.)

fiction (n.)
fabrication, invention, myth, romance, apologue, falsehood, legend, novel, story, fable
Hers is a world of fiction that she has created for herself.

fierce (adj.)
ferocious, furious, raging, uncultivated, violent, fiery, impetuous, savage, untrained, wild, intense, unmerciful
The fierce thunders sound like music to my ears.

financial (adj.)
fiscal, monetary, pecuniary
Every member of this family has to take financial responsibility.

fine (adj., n., adv. & v.)
beautiful, excellent, polished, small, exquisite, pure, smooth, clear, refined, splendid, handsome, sensitive, keen, sharp, subtle, delicate, minute, slender, elegant, nice, slight
There was no need to stay over; the dinner and the movies had been fine. (adj.)
In the painting, her fine-drawn body stood out. (adv.)
You have to pay the fine for breaking the traffic rules. (n.)
I was fined for breaking the traffic rules. (v.)

fire (n. & v.)
blaze, burn, combustion, conflagration, flame, arouse, evoke
There was a sudden fire in the building due to someone's negligence. (n.)
The boss fired the lethargic employee. (v.)

flock (n. & v.)
bevy, covey, group, herd, lot, set, brood, drove, hatch, litter, pack, swarm
We received a flock of fan letters after our first show. (n.)
Tourists flocked to the shrine where the statue was said to have shed tears. (v.)

fluctuate (v.)
hesitate, swerve, vacillate, veer, oscillate, vary, waver

The stock market seems to be really unstable and so it fluctuates.

fluid (n. & adj.)
liquid, runny, smooth
A substance that is fluid at room temperature and pressure is known as a fluid. (n.)
The UK does not seem to be a fluid society, as they behave in an elitist way. (adj.)

follow (v.)
accompany, comply, come after, go after, obey, pursue, attend, copy, observe, result, chase, practise, succeed
Please follow the guide through the museum.
I am giving these instructions for the last time; make sure that you follow what I am saying.

food (n.)
aliment, feed, nourishment, sustenance, diet, fodder, nutriment, forage, nutrition, victuals
For a human being to sustain himself, he needs food and drink.

formidable (adj.)
dangerous, redoubtable, terrible, tremendous, unnerving
The army of the nation posed as a formidable presence to the enemy.

fortification (n.)
castle, citadel, fastness, fort, fortress, stronghold, munition
The art of strengthening defences is called fortification.
To win a war, fortification is necessary.

fortitude (n.)
courage, endurance, heroism, resolution, bravery
Fortitude is a requisite in the arts of fighting a war.

fortunate (adj.)
favoured, lucky, prosperous, successful, blessed
He made a fortunate decision to go to that reputed college.

fraud (n.)
deceit, duplicity, swindle, treason, cheat, deception, imposition, swindling, cheating, dishonesty, treachery, trick, crime
What he did clearly was fraud with the bank

by supplying them fabricated accounts.

friendly (adj.)
accessible, companionable, genial, affable, hearty, sociable, affectionate, cordial, kind, social, amicable, favourable, tender, brotherly, fond, loving, well-disposed
The host and the hostess were friendly as they attended to everyone with utmost warmth.

friendship (n.)
affection, comity, esteem, goodwill, amity, consideration, favour, love, attachment, devotion, friendliness, regard
The friendship between them was exemplary, as they almost never fought.

frighten (v.)
affright, dismay, scare, alarm, browbeat, daunt, intimidate, terrify, terrorise, horrify, spook
The stranger who hangs around my house frightens me.

frugality (n.)
economise, parsimony, saving, sparing, miserliness, scrimping, thriftiness, parsimoniousness, prudence, frugalness
Frugality is something which has both negative and positive connotations.

□

G

garrulous (adj.)
chattering, loquacious, talkative, verbose, talky, chatty, gabby
Some people without realising are garrulous.

gender (n.)
sex, sexuality
They were so excited to have the kid that they never wanted to know the gender of the baby.

general (adj., v. & n.)
common, familiar, ordinary, universal, commonplace, popular, customary, habitual, prevalent, everyday, normal, public
One's general knowledge has to be in place to win this contest. (adj.)
He generalled in the army, and won the war. (v.)
He served as a general in the army. (n.)

generous (adj.)
bountiful, free, liberal, noble, chivalrous, free-handed, magnanimous, open-handed, disinterested, free-hearted, munificent, lavish
He gave the charitable institution a generous donation for the betterment of the kids living there.

genius (n.)
talent, mastermind, champion, virtuoso, prodigy
Einstein undoubtedly was a genius.

get (v.)
achieve, attain, gain, procure, secure, acquire, earn, obtain, receive, win, become, buy
We have to get him to a hospital, or he won't survive.
Did you get my question?

gift (n. & v.)
benefaction, boon, bribe, grant, largess, bequest, bounty, donation, present
She received many gifts

on her birthday. (n.)
Let's gift him a travel package for his anniversary. (v.)

give (v.)
bestow, communicate, deliver, grant, cede, confer, furnish, impart, supply
We give money to the charity to make children's lives better.
The fugitive gave himself up to his pursuers.

govern (v.)
command, curb, influence, mould, reign over, rule, control, direct, manage, reign, restrain, sway, regulate, order
He needs to govern the nation in a better way, or it will go to the dogs.

graceful (adj.)
beautiful, sophisticated, poised, elegant, refined, svelte
She looked so graceful in that dress tonight.

grief (n.)
affliction, melancholy, regret, sorrow, trouble, distress, mourning, sadness, tribulation, woe
It was a matter of great grief to her due to the loss of her friend.

grit (n.)
courage, valour, bravery, fortitude, resoluteness, resolve, toughness, spirit, intrepidity dauntlessness, tenacity, determination, firmness, hardihood, fearlessness
Paragliding requires more grit than you might think.

grow (v.)
flourish, develop, increase, expand, spread, multiply, burgeon, thrive, prosper, mature, ripen, bloom, flower, blossom, fructify
The seeds she had planted grew very slowly.

gruesome (adj.)
ghastly, repugnant, horrible, horrendous, grisly, revolting, repulsive, loathsome, grim, grotesque, macabre, abominable, frightening, fearsome, shocking, awful
The gruesome murder was a reminder of our lost faith in humanity.

guess (v.)
conjecture, estimate, hypothesise, speculate,

postulate
We guessed that the hero might die at the end of the movie.

guidance (n.)
leadership, direction, control, charge, handling, counsel, advice, instruction
The company was lost under his guidance.

guilty (adj.)
responsible, culpable, blameworthy, at fault, delinquent, wrong, offending
The guilty is going to be sent behind bars.

gullible (adj.)
innocent, simple, credulous, naive, unsuspecting, unwary, wide-eyed, inexperienced, immature
I cannot believe that she could be this gullible.

gurgle (v.)
bubble, burble, babble, ripple, splash, murmur, purl
The cool brook gurgled silently through the meadow.

gust (n.)
puff, blow, wind, breeze, blast
A gust of wind blew her scarf off.

gyrate (v.)
rotate, spin, revolve, turn round, whirl, twirl, swirl
The dancers were gyrating on the dance floor.

□

habit (n.)
custom, habitude, routine, system, use, fashion, practise, rule, usage, wont
Smoking is a deadly habit and should be shunned by all means.

happen (v.)
bechance, chance, fall out, supervene, befall, come to pass, occur, take place, betide, fall, encounter
All of us were astounded as to what was really happening.

happiness (n.)
delight, gladness, pleasure, bliss, ecstasy, gratification, rapture, cheer, enjoyment, joy, rejoicing, felicity, merriment, gaiety, mirth, triumph
The feeling that I experienced after climbing that mountain can be called happiness.

happy (adj.)
cheering, gay, lucky, rejoiced, blissful, cheery, glad, merry, rejoicing, blithe, delighted, jocund, mirthful, smiling, blithesome, delightful, jolly, pleased, sprightly, joyful, prosperous, felicitous, joyous, rapturous
It was such a happy event for him to see his daughter walk for the first time.

harmony (n.)
accord, accordance, consonance, union, agreement, unison, amity, consent, unanimity, unity, concord
The ideal state of existing in this world would be when all of us live in complete harmony.

harvest (v. & n.)
crop, harvest-home, ingathering, result, fruit, harvesting, return, growth, produce, harvest-feast, harvest-time, product, harvest-

festival, increase, reaping, yield
We have to harvest the wheat before it starts to spoil. (v.)
The harvest this year was the best that we have had in years. (n.)

hatred (n.)
abhorrence, detestation, hostility, rancour, anger, dislike, ill-will, repugnance, animosity, enmity, malevolence, resentment, antipathy, grudge, malice, revenge, aversion, hate, malignity, spite, loathing, despisal, abomination
The hatred in his heart for her is never going to go away.

have (n. & v.)
hold, occupy, own, possess
They have a beautiful family. (n.)
I have a feeling that your interview is going to go fantastically well. (v.)

hazard (n. & v.)
accident, chance, danger, jeopardy, risk, casualty, contingency, fortuity, peril
Smoking cigarettes and drinking alcohol are health hazards. (n.)
I am not going to hazard my goodwill for no cause. (v.)

healthy (adj.)
hale, hygienic, sanitary, vigorous, healthful, salubrious, sound, well, hearty, strong, wholesome
My priority is to stay fit and healthy.

help (n. & v.)
abet, befriend, foster, succour, aid, cooperate, second, support, assist, encourage, stand by, sustain, uphold
I am going to help her in her fashion enterprise with money. (v.)
With so much going on in his life, I think he might need help in the form of therapy. (n.)

heretic (n.)
dissenter, heresiarch, non-conformist, schismatic, iconoclastic, misbeliever, outcast, recusant
The people who bring about revolutions in the society are bound to be heretics of sorts.

heterogeneous (adj.)
unhomogeneous, conglomerate, miscellaneous, mixed, variant, dissimilar, non-homogeneous, various
The population of India is vast and heterogeneous.

hide (v. & n.)
bury, cover, entomb, overwhelm, suppress, cloak, disguise, inter, screen, veil, conceal, dissemble, mask, blot out
We have to hide the cash in the house as it is not safe. (v.)
The hide of the buffalo is used to make bags, and this cruel practice needs to be stopped. (n.)

high (adj., adv. & n.)
elevated, exalted, noble, steep, towering, eminent, lofty, proud, tall, uplifted, prominent
The money that he demanded for that dress was a high price. (adj.)
People who live high can be termed as elitists. (adv.)
This time the summer temperatures reached an all-time high. (n.)

hinder (v. & adj.)
baffle, clog, foil, obstruct, balk, counteract, frustrate, oppose, stay, bar, delay, hamper, prevent, stop, impede, resist, thwart, encumber, interrupt, block
A jealous person always makes efforts to hinder the others in their progress. (v.)
The hinder part of the animal's carcass was more rotten. (adj.)

history (n.)
account, biography, record, chronicle, register, archive, memoir, annals, narrative
We need to be aware about the history of the world to understand it in a better way.

holy (n. & adj.)
blessed, devoted, hallowed, saintly, consecrated, divine, sacred, sanctum, sacrosanct
He has holy powers which can be witnessed in the miracles he has done. (adj.)
This place is holy, and not everyone is allowed to enter here. (n.)

home (n., v., adv. & adj.)
abode, dwelling, habitation, hearthstone, domicile, fireside, hearth, house, residence, place
She doesn't have a home to go to. (n.)
We like to home people who do not have a home. (v.)
In my home town, people are concerned about each other. (adj.)
After the game, the children brought friends home for supper. (adv.)

honest (adj.)
candid, frank, ingenuous, true, genuine, trustworthy, fair, good, sincere, trusty, faithful, honourable, straightforward, upright, reliable
I want your honest opinion regarding this dress.

horizontal (n. & adj.)
even, flat, level, plain, plane
This object is horizontal. (n.)
Let's look at the horizontal surface of this object. (adj.)

humane (adj.)
benevolent, compassionate, humanist, benignant, forgiving, kind, sympathetic, charitable, gentle, kind-hearted, tender, clement, gracious, merciful
His was a humane gesture towards Peter, as he offered him food.

hunt (v. & n.)
chase, hunting, inquisition, pursuit, search
The detectives hunted the suspect until they found her. (v.)
The hunt for food is necessary for the survival of every being. (n.)

hypocrisy (n.)
formalism, pretense, sanctimony, cant, pharisaism, sanctimoniousness, sham, dissimulation
It is the hypocrisy of the upper classes that seem to care about lower classes.

hypocrite (n.)
cheat, deceiver, dissembler, pretender, dissimulator, phoney
He in all his seriousness

and concern is a hypocrite.

hypothesis (n.)
conjecture, scheme, supposition, system, guess, speculation, surmise, theory, possibility, surmisal
A scientific hypothesis that survives experimental testing becomes a scientific theory.

□

idea (n.)

design, impression, plan, archetype, fancy, judgement, purpose, belief, fantasy, model, notion, supposition, concept, image, opinion, theory, conception, imagination, pattern, thought

His was not a path-breaking idea; he could have definitely done better.

He has the idea that all of us don't like him, and that is really not the case.

ideal (adj. & n.)

archetype, model, idea, original, pattern, prototype, standard

A work of literature may be typical of its period in ideal content. (adj.)

This situation seems ideal for all of us. (n.)

idiocy (n.)

amentia, fatuity, foolishness, incapacity, folly, imbecility, senselessness, stupidity, retardation

It is the sheer idiocy of Molly that she does not want a divorce.

idle (adj., n. & v.)

inactive, inert, slothful, unoccupied, indolent, lazy, sluggish, unemployed, vacant, loaf

These are idle fears of yours which are not going to help you. (adj.)

The car engine was running at idle. (n.)

He idled in bed all morning. (v.)

ignorant (adj.)

ill-informed, unenlightened, unlearned, untaught, illiterate, uninformed, unlettered, untutored, uneducated, uninstructed

Do not mind him, as he is an ignorant man.

imagination (n.)

fancy, fantasy, phantasy,

resource, dream
Children are mesmerised by the works of imagination.

immediately (adv.)
at once, presently, straightway, directly, instantly, right away, forthwith, now, right off, without delay, instantaneously
She was targeting him and he immediately retorted.

immerse (v.)
bury, dip, douse, duck, immerge, plunge, sink, submerge
The object is immersed in water to see if it is buoyant.

imminent (adj.)
impending, threatening, approaching
All the travellers were in imminent danger.

impediment (n.)
bar, clog, encumbrance, obstacle, barrier, difficulty, hindrance, obstruction, deterrent, check
The snow on the mountain posed to be an impediments for the mountaineers.

impudence (n.)
assurance, impertinence, intrusiveness, presumption, boldness, incivility, officiousness, rudeness, effrontery, forwardness, insolence, pertness, sauciness
The impudence of a subordinate to a superior is frowned upon.

incongruous (adj.)
absurd, ill-matched, inharmonious, conflicting, inapposite, contradictory, inappropriate, mismatched, contrary, incommensurable, mismatched, discordant, incompatible, discrepant, inconsistent, unsuitable, unfitting
The illustrations were incongruous with the theme of the book.

induction (n.)
deduction, inference, elicitation, evocation
He was ordered to report for induction into the company.

industrious (adj.)
active, busy, employed, occupied, assiduous, diligent, engaged, sedulous, tireless, untiring, hardworking
These industrious people must have higher income.

industry (n.)
application, diligence, labor, persistence, assiduity, effort, pains, attention, exertion, patience, constancy, intentness, perseverance, sedulousness
Indian industry is making increased use of computers to control production.

infinite (adj. & n.)
illimitable, limitless, unconditioned, boundless, immeasurable, unfathomable, countless, innumerable, numberless, unlimited, eternal, interminable, unbounded
I can give you an infinite number of reasons to not trust that man. (adj.)
If you look at the sky, you can see the boundless regions of the infinite. (n.)

influence (n. & v.)
draw, induce, move, stir, compel, drive, incite, instigate, persuade, sway, dispose, excite, incline, lead, prompt, urge
Her wishes had a great influence on his outlook. (n.)
He influenced her into giving him all her money. (v.)

inherent (adj.)
innate, native, indwelling, inseparable, natural, immanent, infixed, internal, inborn, ingrained, intrinsic, inbred, inhering, inwrought
We could have seen the infirmities inherent in our argument.

injury (n.)
blemish, hurt, loss, damage, impairment, mischief, wrong, detriment, harm, wound, trauma
The injury to the building structure by fire was irrevocable.

injustice (n.)
grievance, injury, unfairness,

unrighteousness, iniquity, unjustness
This act of his was a grave injustice committed to the community.

innocent (adj. & n.)
blameless, inoffensive, spotless, clean, harmless, pure, stainless, clear, immaculate, right, upright, faultless, innocuous, righteous, guileless, sinless, virtuous
The principle that one is innocent until proved guilty is an old one. (adj.)
He is innocent. (n.)

inquisitive (adj.)
curious, meddlesome, peeping, scrutinising, inquiring, prying, searching, intrusive, questioning
Some people are inquisitive about trifles.

insanity (n.)
frenzy, madness, mania, craziness, derangement, lunacy, dementedness, unreasonability
She is so obviously in the traps of insanity.

interpose (v.)
arbitrate, intercept, intermeddle, meddle, intercede, interfere, interrupt, mediate
The combatants interposed in the battlefield in a horrifying manner.

involve (v.)
complicate, embroil, implicate, include, entangle, demand, need, require, call for
We had to involve them for the smooth functioning of the factory.

□

J

jealous (adj.)
resentful, grudging, envious, covetous, green-eyed
She is jealous of attention paid to anyone but herself.

jeopardise (v.)
endanger, imperil, threaten, risk, hazard, venture
You may jeopardise our plan if you so otherwise.

jiggle (v.)
joggle, jig, shake, agitate, wiggle, jerk
She loves jiggling about on the dance floor.

job (n.)
work, employment, position, livelihood, career
I need a job like hers.

join (v.)
unite, connect, link, yoke, combine, glue, weld, solder
These two pieces should be joined together.

joke (n.)
jest, witticism, quip, wordplay, pun
Roger knows the funniest jokes around here.

jolt (v.)
jar, shake up, jostle, bump, bounce, jerk
She had to be jolted out of that dumbstruck phase.

journey (n. & v.)
excursion, pilgrimage, transit, trip, expedition, tour, travel, voyage
A journey from Naples to Rome is beautiful. (n.)
They had to journey the oceans to meet for love. (v.)

joy (n.)
pleasure, gratification, satisfaction, happiness, contentment, enjoyment, felicity, elation, bliss, exhilaration, exultation, rapture
We felt joy at seeing the

children playing happily outside.

judge (v. & n.)
arbitrator, justice, referee, umpire, adjudicator, jurist
I judge this chicken to weigh three pounds. (v.)
The judge tried both father and son in separate trials. (n.)

jump (v.)
leap, bound, spring, pounce, hurdle, hop, skip
Dogs were jumping about in the meadow.

juncture (n.)
point, time, moment, stage, period
At this juncture, suggesting a merger seems premature.

junk (n.)
rubbish, waste, litter, debris, scrap, garbage, trash
You have been given the chore to keep the junk outside every morning.

justice (n.)
equity, legality, rightfulness, fairness, integrity, truth, fair play, justness, right, uprightness, faithfulness, law, righteousness, virtue, honour, lawfulness
The justice of the king for the oppressed has been known in this area.

justify (v.)
vindicate, legitimise, legalise, rationalise, substantiate, defend, support, uphold, validate, warrant
How can you justify hoarding all that black money?

juvenile (adj. & n.)
young, youthful, under-age, minor, immature, adolescent, childish, puerile
Writing on walls of building is juvenile behaviour. (adj.)
The police has arrested a juvenile for theft. (n.)

□

keen (adj.)
enthusiastic, zealous, devoted, ardent, fervent, passionate, eager
They are keen watchers of foreign films.

keep (v. & n.)
carry, hold, preserve, retain, carry on, detain, maintain, protect, support, celebrate, fulfill, obey, refrain, sustain, guard, restrain, withhold
Keep in mind that this has to be kept clean. (v.)
Each child was expected to pay for their keep. (n.)

kick (v.)
boot, punt
The basic aim in soccer is to kick the ball into the back of the net.

kill (v. & n.)
assassinate, dispatch, massacre, put to death, slay, butcher, execute, murder, slaughter, wipe out
This man killed several people when he tried to rob a bank. (v.)
The pilot reported two kills during the mission. (n.)

kin (adj. & n.)
affinity, blood, descent, kind, race, alliance, consanguinity, family, kindred, relationship
He's kin to the River family. (n.)
She is a kin relative to their family. (adj.)

kindness (n.)
warm-heartedness, graciousness, goodness, benevolence, benignity, humanity, generosity, philanthropy, compassion
He appreciated the kindness shown to him by strangers.

king (n.)
prince, majesty, sovereign, monarch, ruler, regent, sovereign, suzerain

The king was worshipped as god in the early times.

kiss (v.)
osculate, peck, smack
I kissed her on the head.

knack (n.)
genius, intuition, talent, gift, skill
He has a knack for saying the right thing.

knit (v.)
join, fasten, weave, interweave, interlace, bind, unite, tie up
She knits all her sweaters.

knock (v.)
strike, hit, rap, thwack, whack, bang, tap
She knocked the stalker on the head with her walking-stick.

know (v.)
understand, comprehend, grasp, acquain, aware, cognizance
I know five languages.

knowledge (n.)
erudition, learning, recognition, experience, cognition, information, cognizance, intelligence, perception, wisdom, comprehension
The present state of knowledge is deplorable in the university system.

knowledgeable (adj.)
aware, informed, well-acquainted, cognizant, enlightened, expert, knowing, well-educated, erudite, learned, intelligent, wise, sagacious
Mr. Sinha is one of the most knowledgeable people I have ever met.

kudos (n.)
raise, acclaim, glory, applause, laudation, acclamation, accolade
They got a lot of kudos for their performance at the theatre.

□

L

language (n.)
expression, patois, vernacular, dialect, idiom, speech, diction, tongue, words, nomenclature
It is difficult to communicate with them as they don't speak our language.

large (adj., n. & adv.)
abundant, gigantic, ample, colossal, grand, massive, big, commodious, great, spacious, broad, considerable, huge, vast, bulky, enormous, immense, wide, capacious
His grandfather had a large and generous spirit. (adj.)
Only large fits him; please get him that. (n.)
From a distance, we could see the ship sailing large. (adv.)

law (n.)
canon, legislation, principle, code, edict, mandate, regulation, command, order, rule, commandment, ordinance, statute, decree, jurisprudence
There are several laws against the abuse of women and children.

liberty (n.)
emancipation, freedom, independence, license, autonomy
In a democracy, people are at a liberty to make their own decisions.

light (n., v., adv. & adj.)
blaze, gleam, glow, shimmer, shine, flare, glimmer, incandescence, flash, glistening, luster, sparkle, flicker, glistering, scintillation, twinkle, glare, glitter, sheen, twinkling (n.)
airy, light-weight, low density, floaty (adj. & adv.)
burn, ignite, illumine,

flame, fire up, light up (v.)
After walking on the dark road, he stepped into the light. (n.)
Everyone in the party wanted to light a cigarette. (v.)
Only some experienced travellers travel light. (adv.)
The bag could only take a light load. (adj.)

likely (adj. & adv.)
conceivable, liable, probable, possible, credible, conjectural, presumable, reasonable, potential
The broken wall in the house is likely to crumble. (adj.)
It seems likely that he would come. (adv.)

listen (v.)
attend, hark, harken, hear, heed, list
We listen for what we expect or desire to hear.

literature (n.)
belles-lettres, literary productions, publications, books, literary works, writings
He did a course in American literature.

load (n. & v.)
burden, charge, encumbrance, pack, cargo, clog, freight, lading, weight (n.)
lade, laden, load up (v.)
The system collapsed under the excessive load. (n.)
All of us should load our bags on the train. (v.)

loathsome (adj.)
detestable, abhorrent, odious, hateful, disgusting, abominable, despicable, contemptible, repulsive, repugnant, nauseating, sickening, revolting
His loathsome presence wasn't wanted there.

local (adj.)
neighbourhood, neighbouring, nearby, close by, adjoining
He works for a local electrician.

lock (n. & v.)
bar, catch, fastening, hook, bolt, clasp, hasp, latch, shut away, interlock, put away
We should put a lock on that door. (n.)
They had to be locked

inside because of the situation outside. (v.)

lofty (adj.)
tall, high, elevated, towering, soaring, exalted, majestic, imposing, grand, magnificent, noble, regal, imperial, blue-blooded, thoroughbred, aristocratic
Milton uses a lofty literary form such as an epic to write.

logic (n.)
reasoning, deduction, dialectics, ratiocination, sense, judgement, wisdom
His decision defies logic.

lonely (adj.)
single, solitary, sole, lone, one, unaccompanied, alone
A lonely human being would get depressed easily.

look (n. & v.)
behold, inspect, see, view, gaze, regard, stare, descry, glance, scan, survey, watch, observe, eye (v.)
appearance, expression, face (n.)
She was looking at him with admiration. (v.)
He had a weird look after I said that to him. (n.)

loose (adj.)
unattached, unconnected, detached, free, unsecured, unfastened
I have a loose tooth. The vacuum cleaner will pick up any loose bits.

loss (n.)
deprivation, bereavement, privation, denial, sacrifice, forfeiture, disappearance
For the family, it was a huge loss.

lost (adj.)
gone, departed, vanished, strayed, missing, mislaid, misplaced, irrecoverable
The airline told me that my bag was lost.

love (v. & n.)
affection, regard, attachment, devotion, liking, tenderness, attraction, fondness, cherishment, admiration, infatuation
I love reading books that are dramatic. (v.)
She was in love with him,

but things turned bitter later on. (n.)

loyalty (n.)
faithfulness, fidelity, devotion, allegiance, trustworthiness, steadfastness, firmness, reliability, stability, dedication, constancy
The loyalty of our soldiers cannot be questioned.

lovely (adj.)
pretty, handsome, attractive, comely, captivating, alluring, enticing, bewitching, ravishing, gorgeous, beautiful, beauteous, pulchritudinous
He has two lovely daughters.

ludicrous (adj.)
ridiculous, laughable, absurd, farcical, nonsensical, preposterous, asinine, foolish, silly, crazy, comical
It is a ludicrous argument.

lull (n.)
pause, interlude, intermission, interval, break, hiatus, interruption
After a brief lull, the hurricane resumed its ferocity.

luminous (adj.)
shiny, bright, illuminated, radiant, alight, resplendent, gleaming, glistening, sparkling, dazzling
The moon looked like a luminous beauty.

lunacy (n.)
madness, insanity, dementia, craziness, derangement, psychosis, mania
Formerly, it was believed that lunacy is usually found in women.

lure (v.)
tempt, attract, coax, seduce, draw in, entice, decoy, charm, persuade, allure
He lured me into the trap of believing that he loved me.

lust (n.)
sensuality, libido, sexuality, lustfulness, concupiscence
The young wish to satisfy their lust; no matter whatever it takes.

lustrous (adj.)
glossy, shiny, shined, polished, burnished
The furniture has a lustrous finish.

lusty (adj.)
vigorous, healthy, strong, energetic, robust, lively, lascivious
He has a lusty gaze.

luxury (n.)
opulence, splendour, grandeur, extravagance, magnificence, richness
He had been living a life of luxury in India.

□

M

make (v. & n.)
become, fabricate, manufacture, construct, fashion, create, force, perform, do, frame, reach, cause, get, render, compel, establish, compose, shape, constitute
Shakespeare is known for making sonnets and plays. (v.)
How much do you make in a month? (v.)
What make of truck is that? (n.)

marriage (n.)
conjugal union, espousal, matrimony, nuptials, spousal relationship, wedding, wedlock
Marriage between two persons conventionally means a lifetime of commitment.

masculine (adj. & n.)
male, manful, manlike, manly, mannish, virile
She also has that masculine quality in her personality. (adj.)
He is so masculine. (n.)

massacre (v. & n.)
butchery, carnage, havoc, slaughter, kill, murder, slay, execution
The Jews had to be massacred after Hitler declared his rule. (v.)
The massacre in Germany is the biggest in the history of the world. (n.)

meddlesome (adj.)
intrusive, meddling, obtrusive, officious, interfering
Her meddlesome attitude is what I don't like about her.

melody (n.)
harmony, music, symphony, unison, tune
He was humming a melody from Schubert.

memory (n.)
recollection, remembrance,

reminiscence, retrospect, retrospection
She had an amazing memory when she was a girl.

mercy (n.)
favour, kindness, mildness, benignity, forbearance, lenience, pardon, forgiveness, pity, gentleness, lenity, tenderness, compassion, clemency
The mercy of God towards sinners is the example of his godliness.

meter (n. & v.)
euphony, measure, rhythm, verse
Many poets write their verses in meters of several kinds. (n.)
Let's meter the flow of the water. (v.)

mind (n. & v.)
brain, reason, consciousness, intellect, sense, thought, disposition, intelligence, understanding, judgement, discernment
His mind wandered to the thoughts of love. (n.)
One should mind the advice of elders. (v.)

minute (n. & v. & adj.)
diminutive, little, slender, comminuted, particular, small, fine, precise, tiny, detailed
It will only take me a minute to download the air ticket. (n.)
Let's minute the meeting. (v.)
The officers did a minute inspection of the school's premises. (adj.)

misfortune (n.)
adversity, ill-fortune, ruin, affliction, disaster, distress, misadventure, stroke, blow, failure, mischance, trial, calamity, hardship, misery, tribulation, harm, mishap, trouble
It was a sheer misfortune that the bus fell into the river.

mission (n.)
duty, purpose, job, work, business, pursuit, aim, objective
The mission to colonise was a threat to other civilisations.

mistaken (adj.)
wrong, amiss, incorrect, erring, inaccurate, out of order

I was mistaken that girl for another girl.

misunderstand (v.)
misconceive, misconstrue, misinterpret, misapprehend, misread, misjudge
He understood your words but misunderstood your meaning.

mitigate (v.)
reduce, abate, lessen, decrease, relieve, alleviate, remit, assuage, allay, slacken
The pain was mitigated by taking a medicine.

mixture (n.)
assortment, amalgamation, combination, intermingling, composite, blend, mix
The dress was a mixture of many incompatible styles.

mob (n. & v.)
masses, throng, rabble, crowd, lower classes, populace, the vulgar, gangdom, gangland
The police tried to stop the mob from breaking in. (n.)
People mobbed the performance in the concert. (v.)

model (n., v. & adj.)
archetype, original, representation, pattern, standard, design, imitation, prototype, type, example, prototype, exhibit
The car was a very old model. (n.)
She has to model the latest fashion, or she will lag behind. (v)
All these citizens cleaning the roads are model citizens. (adj.)

modern (adj.)
current, contemporary, novel, present-day, latest, new
Sally is too modern for her times.

modesty (n.)
reserve, timidity, bashfulness, coyness, shyness
She is known all around for her modesty.

moist (adj.)
damp, wettish, dewy, dank, humid, clammy, steamy, soggy
His hands are always

moist because of his nervousness.

monarch (n.)
ruler, sovereign, king, empress, emperor, czar, suzerain
The monarch is omnipotent.

monotonous (adj.)
banal, boring, dull, tiresome, humdrum, soporific, wearisome, prosaic, dry, uninteresting
Existence is monotonous for everyone.

monstrous (adj.)
horrible, horrendous, ugly, nightmarish, dreadful, heinous, grisly, grotesque, ghoulish, fiendish, barbarous, savage, inhuman, brutish, beastly
What Dr. Frankenstein created was monstrous being.

mood (n.)
attitude, disposition, nature, temper, frame of mind, spirit, atmosphere
After her divorce, she is never in a good mood.

moot (adj.)
debatable, arguable, undecided, undetermined, controversial, doubtful, disputable, questionable, contestable, contested, unsettled, unresolved
Draupadi's question in the assembly hall was a moot point.

money (n.)
bills, cash, funds, property, bullion, coin, capital, currency, notes, wealth, bucks, dough
She needs money desperately for her daughter's operation.

morale (n.)
spirit, esprit de corps, disposition, attitude, confidence, self-esteem
The morale of the team was low after their first loss.

moribund (adj.)
dying, failing, fading, ending, declining, weak, waning, stagnant
He's a moribund patient, and chances are he won't survive.

morose (adj.)
dogged, ill-natured, splenetic, churlish, gloomy, sulky, gruff,

snappish, sullen, ill-humoured, sour
He always had a morose and unsociable manner.

mortal (adj.)
human, temporal, transient, temporal, ephemeral, fleshly, earthly, worldly, perishable
Human beings are mortal.

mortify (v.)
humiliate, shame, humble, embarrass, abash, crush, deflate, bring down, degrade, chasten
He was mortified to know that his swindling had been discovered by the authorities.

motif (n.)
theme, idea, concept, leitmotif, pattern, figure, device, ornament, element
The same motif has been used for several purposes in the novel.

motion (n. & v.)
act, change, movement, transition, action, passage, transit, move
Both of them were in a state of steady motion. (n.)
She motioned her wish to speak. (v.)

motive (n.)
motivation, stimulus, influence, cause, reason, rationale, purpose, aim, intent, objective, goal, end
I am sure there are some hidden motives behind this move.

motto (n.)
maxim, proverb, saying, adage, aphorism, slogan, byword, principle, rule, precept
Our motto is to live and let live.

mountainous (adj.)
huge, towering, high, enormous, immense, formidable, mighty, monumental, staggering
It was a mountainous task for all of us.

mourn (v.)
bemoan, deplore, lament, regret, bewail, grieve
He is mourning his dead mother.

mouthpiece (n.)
embouchure, spokesperson, agent,

representative, mediator, delegate
He is always quoted through his mouthpiece, never directly.

mow (v.)
cut down, scythe, trim, shear
My father mows the garden in the morning.

mull (v.)
ponder, consider, think over, evaluate, deliberate over, reflect upon, review, examine, contemplate, meditate upon, chew over, ruminate over
I have taken some time to mull over what you said.

murder (n.)
homicide, manslaughter, killing, slaying, assassination
The terrorists are known for the murder of thousands of people.

murky (adj.)
dark, gloomy, threatening, overcast, cloudy dismal, dreary, grim, shady, shadowy
There was something murky in his eyes.

muscular (adj.)
sinewy, brawny, burly, powerful, rugged, husky, robust, athletic, sturdy
He built his muscular physique after months of hard work.

mushy (adj.)
soft, pulpy, squashy, squidgy, spongy, swampy, boggy
The fruit was overripe and mushy.

muster (v.)
come together, assemble, convoke, convene, mobilize, rally, gather, marshal, summon
I mustered up enough courage to sleep in the dark.

mute (adj. & v.)
silent, dumb, speechless, voiceless, tight-lipped, taciturn, reserved, quiet (adj.)
silence, muffle, stifle, subdue, suppress, quieten, hush, tone down (v.)
The assailants muted the victim. (v.)
She remained mute after the disaster. (adj.)

mutilate (v.)
maim, disfigure, cripple, lame, butcher, dismember, amputate, hack off, cut off, tear off
The prisoners of war were mutilated to make them speak up.

mutiny (n.)
revolt, rebellion, revolution, subversion, insurgence, insurrection, uprising
The rebels are planning a mutiny against the government.

mutual (adj.)
common, correlative, interchangeable, joint, reciprocal, complementary
They have mutual respect for each other and that is worth admiring.

mysterious (adj.)
inexplicable, inscrutable, secret, dark, enigmatical, mystical, unfathomable, hidden, obscure, unfathomed, incomprehensible, occult, unknown, deep
On the surface of the walls, we discovered some mysterious signs.

mystify (v.)
fool, hoax, confuse, confound, bewilder, stump, puzzle, baffle, flummox, stump
We were completely mystified by the cryptic signs in the cave.

myth (n.)
legend, fable, allegory, parable, tradition, saga, epic
There are many myths in our past.

□

N

nag (v.)
annoy, irritate, irk, pester, criticise, scold, harass, vex, henpeck
She nags him all the time.

naive (adj.)
ingenuous, innocent, credulous, childlike, inexperienced, unworldly, unsuspecting, gullible, guileless, simple-minded
Sally is too naive for her age.

naked (adj.)
sun-clothed, undraped, bare, exposed, stripped, undressed, unclad, uncovered, bare, nude
I could not believe that he jumped into the pool naked.

name (n.)
designation, label, appellation, term, tag
I really like her name; it means something profound.

nap (v.)
doze, catnap, snooze
I nap every afternoon.

narcotic (adj.)
soporific, sedative, sleep-inducing, opiate, dulling, numbing, anaesthetic, stupefacient, tranquillising
Most narcotic drugs are not easily available.

narration (n.)
telling, unfolding, recounting, chronicling, recitation, description, portrayal, detailing, revelation, speaking
His narration was not convincing and could have been better.

narrative (n.)
story, tale, chronicle, account, report, record, history, statement
The narrative of his was absolutely fascinating.

narrow (adj.)
constricted, slender, slim, thin, restricted

The narrow passage made it difficult to pass through.

nasty (adj.)
foul, filthy, dirty, disgusting, nauseating, revolting, horrible, loathsome, repugnant, vile, odious, obnoxious, nauseous, sickening, rancid, noxious
The nasty stench of rotten fruits forced us to step outside.

nation (n.)
country, state, land, political entity, polity, territory
The idea of nation is what keeps people together.

native (adj.)
innate, natural, inherent, inherited, hereditary, intrinsic, domestic, local, home-grown, indigenous, autochthonous, aboriginal
Early in life, Holly showed a native capacity dancing.
The native people are illiterate in this area.

natural (adj.)
ordinary, common, normal, standard, regular, usual, routine, habitual, typical, reasonable
The baby had a natural birth.

nature (n.)
quality, properties, features, character, personality, essence, disposition, temperament
The nature of this compound is still undiscovered.

naughty (adj.)
mischievous, impish, puckish, roguish, devilish, playful, notorious
Children by their very nature are naughty.

nauseate (v.)
sicken, disgust, repel, revolt
Your hypocrisy nauseates me.

navigate (v.)
sail, voyage, cruise, journey; cross, traverse
We were navigating to find that place.

navy (n.)
fleet, flotilla, naval forces, armada
The navy like the army has a huge responsibility.

nearby (adv.)
close by, close at hand, in the vicinity, neighbourhood, about, around
She lives nearby only.

neat (adj.)
tidy, orderly, clean, uncluttered, spick and span, organized, systematic
She keeps her room neat.

nebulous (adj.)
vague, hazy, clouded, unclear, obscure, indistinct, fuzzy, muddy, blurred, indeterminate, murky, dim, foggy
The idea was nebulous and, therefore, could not be executed.

necessary (adj.)
indispensable, essential, required, compulsory, requisite, vital, imperative, needful, important
A good routine is necessary for good health.

need (v.)
require, demand, want, be in want of
This dress needs to be stitched properly.

negative (adj.)
anti, contrary, dissenting, disputatious, argumentative, adversarial, antagonistic, antipathetic
His negative attitude is not going to fetch him anything.

neglect (v.)
disregard, ignore, slight, overlook
Everyone neglected his presence in the class.

negotiate (v.)
deal, bargain, haggle, chaffer, discuss, mediate, consult, parley, talk, transact
We have negotiated with each other for many years.

neighbourhood (n.)
locality, area, region, vicinity, milieu, environs, locale, surroundings
They live in a posh neighbourhood.

nerve (n.)
courage, boldness, bravery, determination, valour, daring, mettle, spirit, fortitude, will, tenacity, grit
It took a lot of nerve

to climb that patch of mountain.

nervous (adj.)
tense, agitated, flustered, disturbed, perturbed, distressed, worried, anxious, fidgety, apprehensive, frightened, fearful, scared
Everyone becomes nervous when one has to go on stage.

neurotic (adj.)
unstable, confused, disordered, distraught, overwrought, anxious, obsessive, deviant
Most people are neurotic about something or another.

never (adv.)
not ever, not at any time, on no occasion, under no circumstances, on no account
Never leave your children alone with strangers.

new (adj.)
novel, unusual, different, fresh, creative, imaginative
We have found a new way of doing old things.

news (n.)
word, information, rumour, gossip, hearsay, scoop
What's the latest news about the situation in Kashmir?

nice (adj.)
pleasant, agreeable, friendly, cordial, warm-hearted, kind, outgoing, charming, genial, delightful, refined, likeable
The couple that has recently moved into the neighbourhood is nice.

niche (n.)
recess, hollow, alcove, nook, place, position
He has finally found a niche for himself as an author.

nifty (adj.)
smart, stylish, modish, chic
I borrowed a nifty dress from my friend.

night (n.)
dark, darkness, blackness, night-time, tenebrosity
Dr. Frankenstein's monster slunk into the night.

nimble (adj.)
agile, lively, active, sprightly, brisk, smart, energetic, rapid, quick, swift, adroit, deft, dexterous
He is nimble as a leopard hunting for prey.

nobility (n.)
nobleness, dignity, grandeur, illustriousness, greatness, leadership, distinction, integrity, excellence, goodness, decency, high-mindedness
The nobility of that man cannot be described.

nod (v.)
greet, acknowledge, recognise, agree, say yes
He nodded to all the suggestions made in the meeting.

noisy (adj.)
loud, deafening, jarring, harsh, piercing, shrill, discordant, unmusical, dissonant, cacophonous, clamorous, blaring, blasting
I could hear nothing over the noisy classroom.

nominate (v.)
choose, select, name, appoint, designate, suggest, offer, submit, recommend, propose
She has been nominated for the presidency.

non-believer (n.)
unbeliever, disbeliever, cynic, doubter, sceptic, freethinker, agnostic, atheist
The number of non-believers in the world is increasing by the day.

nonchalant (adj.)
cool, unexcited, imperturbable, untroubled, unruffled, dispassionate, unemotional, casual, relaxed, at ease
How can people be so nonchalant about other people's problems?

nonconformist (n.)
maverick, rebel, radical, heretic, dissenter, dissident, iconoclast, loner, exception, anomaly, iconoclast
He does everything unusually, and is a nonconformist of sorts.

nondescript (adj.)
indescribable, unclassified, ordinary,

common, commonplace, unremarkable, drab, bland, unexceptional
He was wearing nondescript outfit for the party.

nonplus (v.)
confound, perplex, puzzle, confuse, dismay, baffle, dumbfound, astonish, astound
She was nonplussed to find out his ulterior motives.

nonsense (n.)
rubbish, drivel, gibberish, twaddle, trash, babble, balderdash, bombast, mumbo-jumbo, hogwash, garbage
His talk for the occasion was pure nonsense.

nook (n.)
cranny, recess, niche, corner, cavity, crevice, crack, opening
Flowers grew from the nooks in the wall.

norm (n.)
usual, model, standard, type, normal, pattern, criterion, rule, measure, gauge, yardstick
This washing of feet before you enter a religious place has been the norm for many years.

normal (adj.)
standard, regular, conventional, usual, ordinary, routine, universal, general, common, customary, typical
His way of doing things seems normal but it surely is not.

nosy (adj.)
curious, inquisitive, prying, meddlesome, spying, peeping, eavesdropping
You should mind your own business and don't be so nosy.

notable (adj.)
noteworthy, noted, famous, famed, renowned, illustrious, important, eminent, outstanding, great, distinguished, celebrated, acclaimed
Many notable people were present at the annual convocation.

note (n. & v.)
message, letter, epistle, postcard, fan letter, word, line (n.)

notice, observe, perceive, see, mark, think about, consider, pay attention to, investigate (v.)
I have sent her a note to attend the meeting. (n.)
I have noted how people try to avoid you because of your bad habits. (v.)

nothing (n.)
cipher, zero, nobody, nonentity, naught, nothing at all, no thing, not anything
Nothing that you tell me will be revealed to other people.
There was a time when I had nothing with me.

noticeable (adj.)
discernible, perceivable, recognisable, distinguishable, visible, palpable, manifest, distinct, evident, clear, clear-cut, conspicuous, obvious
I don't think that the scratch on the car is noticeable.

notorious (adj.)
disreputable, dishonourable, disgraceful, infamous, scandalous, naughty, flagrant
He was spotted in public with drug peddler, and that is going to get him a notorious reputation.

nourish (v.)
feed, sustain, support, maintain, keep, provide for, care for, take care of, look after, nurture, nurse
The child seems to be thriving and well nourished.

novel (adj. & n.)
new, unusual, unfamiliar, unconventional, fresh, different, original, creative (adj.)
story, tale, narrative, romance, novella, novelette, best-seller (n.)
I have a novel idea about running the business. (adj.)
She had written a fantastic novel. (n.)

nudge (v.)
poke, elbow, jab, bump, prompt, shove, prod, push
I had to nudge her to keep her mouth shut.

numb (adj.)
benumbed, insensate, dead, deadened, unfeeling, sensationless

My body is numb from the exposure to this cold outside.

nuptial (adj.)

bridal, matrimonial, wedding, spousal, wedded, marital, connubial, conjugal

The nuptial arrangements are not yet complete.

nurse (v.)

care, tend, attend, nurture, foster, coddle, pamper, cherish, preserve

She nursed him throughout the period of his illness.

□

oar (n.)
paddle, scull
We had used all the oars to get out of the storm.

oasis (n.)
haven, refuge, harbour, sanctuary, retreat, resort, sanctum
We were looking for an oasis in the desert.

oath (n.)
vow, avowal, pledge, promise, word, promise, plight, guarantee
He has taken an oath to reveal everything.

obedience (n.)
dutifulness, conformity, yielding, adaptability, agreeability, acquiescence, submissiveness, subservience, docility, passivity
Her obedience is something that everyone praises her for.

obese (adj.)
fat, overweight, stout, fleshy, gross, corpulent, heavy, plump, portly, chubby, paunchy
I sat down next to an obese person who occupied nearly two chairs.

obey (v.)
comply, observe, respect, adhere to, follow, mind, accept, heed
His orders have to be obeyed; otherwise, he becomes angry.

obituary (n.)
necrology, death notice, eulogy
Some people write their own obituary.

object (n.)
thing, tangible, item, entity
The objects are lying all around the place.

objection (n.)
protest, opposition, question, disapproval, remonstrance, stand
The objection was raised the members of the other party.

objective (n.)
target, goal, object, aim, purpose, end, intent, intention, design, ambition
My objective is to run the marathon.

obligate (n.)
oblige, pledge, commit, bind, require
I feel deeply obligated to her for her kindness to our children.

oblique (adj.)
awry, devious, roundabout, indirect, evasive, sly, surreptitious, implied, clandestine, devious, deceptive
She made some oblique comments about the candidate's wife.

obliterate (v.)
erase, expunge, rub out, efface, eradicate, wipe out, delete, eliminate
His name was obliterated from the list after the problem.

oblivion (n.)
blankness, blackness, darkness, obscurity, nothingness, nihility, anonymity
All that fame went into oblivion.

obnoxious (adj.)
revolting, repulsive, repugnant, disgusting, offensive, fulsome, noisome, vile, repellent, nauseous, foul, unsavoury, loathsome, detestable, odious, scurvy, despicable, awful, distasteful, nasty
The issue seems to be completely obnoxious.

obscene (adj.)
shameful, indecent, immodest, risque, vulgar, immoral, amoral, erotic, sensual, ribald, debauched, loose, libertine, dirty, filthy, pornographic, libidinous, lewd, licentious, lecherous, lustful, carnal, lascivious, offensive
This is an obscene movie, which should not be released.

obscure (adj.)
dark, gloomy, sombre, dismal, dusky, black, blurred, veiled, shadowy, hazy, foggy, clouded, nebulous
The obscure drawing on the map was not helpful.

obsequious (adj.)
low, cringing, sycophantish, unctuous,

grovelling, deferential, servile, slavish, subservient, submissive, slimy
He has a throng of obsequious people surrounding him.

observant (adj.)
watchful, alert, attentive, vigilant, mindful, aware, keen, perceptive, sharp
He was observant of all who were there in the party that night.

observe (v.)
obey, abide by, conform to, regard, follow, adhere to, respect, comply
We observed the prohibition against smoking and drinking.

obsession (n.)
fixation, prepossession, passion, mania
Shopping became her constant obsession.

obsolete (adj.)
outdated, passé, dead, outmoded, old, archaic, old-fashioned, discarded, extinct
His ways of clicking photographs has become obsolete now.

obstacle (n.)
impediment, hindrance, obstruction, hurdle, hitch, snag, stumbling-block, barrier, bar
Overcoming obstacles is a part of becoming successful.

obstinate (adj.)
stubborn, dogged, headstrong, pigheaded, single-minded, recalcitrant, obdurate, fixed, inflexible, adamant, unmoving, unyielding, rigid
The person behind that counter seems obstinate.

obstreperous (adj.)
clamorous, noisy, loud, riotous, uproarious, tumultuous, boisterous, rowdy, rumbustious, tempestuous, unruly
The people in the team were getting obstreperous.

obstruct (v.)
block, bar, hamper, slow, impede, hinder, interrupt, delay, stall
He obstructed my way in the college.

obtain (v.)
get, procure, acquire, secure, grasp, capture, buy, purchase, earn, gain
You can obtain many

benefits from this product.

obtrusive (adj.)
intrusive, meddling, officious, meddlesome, importunate, presumptuous, forceful
He pokes his nose in other people's business; he found him obtrusive.

obvious (adj.)
clear, plain, apparent, perceptible, evident, ostensible, pronounced, prominent, glaring, undeniable, unhidden, self-explanatory
It was obvious that she was not going to come back.

occasion (n.)
time, moment, circumstance, incident, occurrence, opportunity, chance, opening
I took the occasion of the inquiry to leave the town.

occult (adj.)
secret, dark, concealed, privy, hidden, obscure, veiled, shrouded, vague, shadowy, mystical, mysterious, cabbalistic, esoteric, recondite
Tarot card reading was kept an occult art for many generations.

occupation (n.)
job, position, post, appointment, employment, vocation, career, field, craft, skill, profession, business, work
Her occupation is that of a typist in that law firm.

occupy (v.)
capture, seize, take possession of, conquer, invade, take over, overrun, garrison, dominate, hold
They occupied a lot of space in the house.

occurrence (n.)
happening, event, incident, phenomenon, matter
Robberies are frequent occurrences in that part of the country.

oddity (n.)
peculiarity, strangeness, unnaturalness, incongruity, eccentricity, extraordinariness, bizarreness, weirdness, unusualness, anomaly
What caught my attention was the oddity of the clothes worn by the students.

odour (n.)
smell, scent, aroma, stench, stink
The odour of rotting fruits overpowered all our senses.

offence (n.)
violation, breach, crime, felony, misdemeanour, transgression, trespass, wrongdoing, sin, misdeed, fault, infringement
His was a grave offence, which could not be neglected.

offer (v.)
proffer, propose, tender, bid
They offered him a great offer, but he refused.

office (n.)
business, organisation, department, firm, house, establishment, company, corporation
I consider my office to be a sacred space.

officious (adj.)
dictatorial, intrusive, meddling, obtrusive, interfering, aggressive, insistent, demanding
Hamish is one of those officious little men who are always ready to give unasked-for advice.

ogle (v.)
leer, eye, make eyes at, gaze at, gawk
The old lecher is always ogling the pretty young secretaries

oily (adj.)
greasy, oleaginous, fatty, adipose, saponaceous, buttery, slippery, slimy, slithery, smooth
This oily dish is not edible.

old (adj.)
elderly, ageing, aged, hoary, superannuated ancient, antiquated
His father is too old to work.

omen (n.)
portent, augury, sign, foretoken, indication, forewarning, premonition, foreshadowing, presage
There are many occurrences that people think of as omens.

ominous (adj.)
foreboding, threatening, fateful, dark, black, menacing, sinister, unpropitious, unfavourable, ill-starred,

inauspicious
There are some things considered to be ominous incidents.

omission (n.)
non-inclusion, omitting, leaving out or off, excluding, eliminating, dropping, skipping; exclusion, exception, deletion, elimination, excision
The omission of his name from the committee was deliberate.

onlooker (n.)
spectator, observer, eyewitness, watcher, viewer, bystander
He was an onlooker when crime took place there.

only (adj.)
sole, single, solitary, lone, exclusive
She is the only one who can focus on several things at the same time.

ooze (n.)
slime, muck, mud, mire, sludge, slush
She stepped into the swampy area and the ooze enveloped her feet.

openly (adv.)
brazenly, brashly, flagrantly, unabashedly, audaciously, frankly, unreservedly, candidly, freely, outspokenly
He openly rejected her advances.

operate (v.)
go, run, perform, work, function, serve, act
We have to operate the machinery keeping in mind its technicalities.

opinion (n.)
belief, judgment, thought, viewpoint, perception, idea, impression, notion, conception
She takes the opinions of the superiors seriously.

opinionated (adj.)
judgemental, obstinate, inflexible, dogmatic, single-minded, obdurate, dictatorial, dogged
She is too opinionated to see the truth in this situation.

opponent (n.)
adversary, contestant, competitor, contender, rival, foe, enemy
Ross is considered to be the strongest opponent.

opportunistic (adj.)
selfish, exploitative, unprincipled
Most of the people in this society are opportunistic.

opportunity (n.)
chance, occasion, opening, possibility, moment, time
Every opportunity that comes our way should be considered seriously.

opposition (n.)
hostility, antagonism, resistance, counteraction, disapproval, objection, antipathy
We have opposition regarding the many steps that our government is going to take.

oppression (n.)
repression, subjugation, subjection, enslavement, persecution, maltreatment, abuse, torture, hardship
Many kinds of oppression are still not revealed to public at large.

optimistic (adj.)
positive, hopeful, expectant, idealistic
She is too optimistic, and sometimes it is not healthy.

option (n.)
choice, selection, alternative, recourse, opportunity, way out
There are not too many options out there for old people.

opulent (adj.)
wealthy, affluent, rich, prosperous, comfortable, luxurious, lavish
The opulent castle was awe-inspiring.

opus (n.)
work, composition, production, oeuvre, creation
Her greatest opus is going to be there in theatres this week.

oration (n.)
speech, declaration, address, lecture, declamation
Steve Jobs has given several orations on the future of Apple Inc.

ordeal (n.)
trial, test, tribulation, hardship, affliction, trouble, suffering, misfortune, adversity, tragedy

The loss of her child was an ordeal for her.

order (n. & v.)
organisation, uniformity, regularity, system, pattern, symmetry, harmony, tidiness, orderliness (n.)
direct, command, instruct, charge, tell, bid, require, enjoin; demand, ordain (v.)
Everything around here has to be in order. (n.)
The umpire ordered the player to get off the field. (v.)

ordinary (adj.)
usual, normal, common, general, routine, typical, habitual, traditional, regular, everyday, familiar
This is an ordinary getup, which would not be good enough for the event.

organism (n.)
structure, body, being, creature
There are numerous kinds of organisms in the world.

organize (v.)
structure, coordinate, systematise, order, arrange, catalogue, codify
We have to organize everything in its said order.

ornamental (adj.)
decorative, beautifying, adorning, garnishing, embellishing
The ornamental display in the wedding could have been avoided.

oscillate (v.)
fluctuate, waver, swing, sway, vacillate
The pendulum of the clock oscillates perfectly.

ostracize (v.)
blacklist, banish, exile, boycott, isolate, segregate, exclude, excommunicate, snub, shun
Carrie has been ostracized at the school because of what she did.

outcome (n.)
result, consequence, end product, effect, upshot
The outcome of this experiment will decide if we are going to use the product.

outcry (n.)
protestation, indignation, uproar, vociferation, clamouring, outburst, howl
This outcry about

pollution is justified, given the present conditions.

outlandish (adj.)
unfamiliar, strange, odd, peculiar, exotic, foreign, alien, different, exceptional, extraordinary, quaint, eccentric, bizarre, weird, fantastic, unusual, unique
His to-do list is one of the most outlandish ones that I have seen till date.

outrageous (adj.)
extravagant, exorbitant, enormous, unreasonable, preposterous, shocking, extreme, exaggerated, intolerable, disgraceful, shameful, scandalous
His outrageous response to the problem was not expected.

outset (n.)
beginning, start, inception, first
At the outset, the piece of writing informs us about the elements in it.

outspoken (adj.)
candid, frank, free, unreserved, straightforward, forthright, uninhibited, blunt, brash
He was always quite outspoken about the things he doesn't appreciate.

ovation (n.)
applause, acclamation, cheering, clapping, laudation
A standing ovation is what everyone desires.

overconfident (adj.)
cocksure, hubristic, swaggering, overbearing, vainglorious
An overconfident person can lead to defeat of the team.

overwhelming (adj.)
overpowering, irresistible, unendurable, unbearable, crushing, formidable
He had an overwhelming sense of shame for what he had said.

owe (v.)
be indebted to
She owes him a lot of money.

owner (n.)
possessor, holder, proprietor
The owner of the property was missing after the murder.

□

pact (n.)
agreement, treaty, alliance, contract, covenant, understanding, arrangement, deal
The countries entered into a pact to counter terrorism.

pageantry (n.)
pomp, ceremony, display, magnificence, extravagance, show, exhibition
The pageantry of the aristocratic households cannot be everyone's privilege.

pain (n.)
hurt, suffering, discomfort, soreness, ache, anguish, agony, affliction, distress, grief, misery
I feel the pain in my hand from exercising too much.

paint (v.)
depict, portray, picture, show, represent, render, draw, characterise, describe
Reporters painted a gory account of the murders.

pal (n.)
friend, comrade, companion, buddy
She has many pals in the class.

palatial (adj.)
luxurious, splendid, stately, opulent, majestic, magnificent, grand
His palatial house is right around the corner.

pale (adj.)
wan, sallow, ashen, pallid, pasty, drained, ghostly, ghastly
His pale was a proof of the depression he was undergoing.

paltry (adj.)
trifling, trivial, petty, small, insignificant, inconsequential, meagre, beggarly, low
We all recognise Denison

for the paltry pedant he is.

pamper (v.)
coddle, indulge, spoil, mollycoddle, pet
The parents pamper their children and spoil them.

panache (n.)
flourish, dash, élan, chic, sophistication, flamboyance, verve, flair, swagger
She can carry off anything she wears with panache.

pandemonium (n.)
bedlam, chaos, turmoil, disorder, tumult, frenzy, uproar
Pandemonium reigned after the building collapsed.

panic (n. & v.)
terror, alarm, fear, fright, dread, hysteria, apprehensiveness, nervousness
A feeling of panic gripped me when I saw the glass falling over my head. (n.)
I panicked just before the exam. (v.)

panoramic (adj.)
sweeping, commanding, extensive, wide, scenic, far-reaching, all-embracing, far-ranging, all-encompassing, bird's-eye
This room has a panoramic view of the sea.

paradise (n.)
heaven, dreamland, Eden
Adam and Eve were banished from the Paradise.

paradox (n.)
contradiction, self-contradiction, incongruity
We inhabit a world of paradoxes.

paragon (n.)
epitome, archetype, model, prototype, quintessence, exemplar
She is a paragon of virtue for what she does for the poor.

paralyse (v.)
immobilise, inactivate, transfix, halt, stop, numb, freeze
The stroke paralysed her body.

paramount (adj.)
pre-eminent, chief, supreme, dominant, main, cardinal, first, primary, principal, essential, vital
It is of paramount importance that we complete the work assigned to us.

paramour (n.)
lover, love, amorist, mistress, concubine
He flaunted about his many paramours in front of everyone.

paraphernalia (n.)
apparatus, accessories, appliances, things, accoutrements, appurtenances, trappings, baggage
They are to bring along their swimming paraphernalia.

parentage (n.)
lineage, ancestry, line, family, descent, origin, bloodline, heritage, roots
People blame parentage for the flaws in a person.

parity (n.)
equality, equivalence, consistency, par, likeness, similarity, analogy, congruity, similitude
Parity of wealth should solve world's problems.

parley (n.)
conference, discussion, dialogue, deliberation, meeting, confabulation
The problem will be fixed at the college department's parley.

parlous (adj.)
perilous, risky, precarious, dangerous, hazardous
These are parlous times world over.

parochial (adj.)
regional, provincial, local, insular, isolated, limited, restricted, narrow-minded, prejudiced
Hers is a parochial view of the world.

parody (n.)
burlesque, lampoon, satire, caricature, mockery, mimicry, spoof, travesty, mockery
What they did to the sequel was a parody of the original movie.

partiality (n.)
prejudice, bias, inclination, favouritism, leaning, preference

The judges were blamed of partiality by the participants.

partisan (n.)
follower, supporter, adherent, backer, champion, enthusiast, fan, zealot
She has always been a partisan of socialism.

partition (n.)
separation, division, splitting, break-up, breaking up, segmentation
The partition of India and Pakistan was imminent.

passenger (n.)
rider, fare, traveller, voyager, commuter
The passengers in the bus were ill-mannered.

passionate (adj.)
ardent, eager, intense, fervid, zealous, earnest, zestful, vehement, impassioned, emotional, animated, spirited, enthusiastic
People are passionate about some things.

passive (adj.)
inactive, inert, motionless, unresponsive, quiet, still, unmoved, impassive, dispassionate
Passive people can also be aggressive at times.

pastiche (n.)
mixture, medley, blend, composite, patchwork, pot-pourri
The dress was a pastiche of different styles.

pastime (n.)
hobby, avocation, recreation, diversion, amusement, entertainment, divertissement
As a pastime, he likes watching movies.

pastoral (adj.)
bucolic, idyllic, tranquil, serene, restful, peaceful, harmonious
Wordsworth is noted for his pastoral poetry.

paternal (adj.)
fatherly, kindly, fond, devoted, loving, patriarchal, patrilineal
His paternal feelings could not be controlled after he saw the baby.

patience (n.)
tolerance, forbearance, restraint, sufferance, submission, resignation

Patience is a treasured virtue.

patriotic (adj.)
nationalistic, loyalist, flag-waving, jingoistic, chauvinistic
Most of the people I know are patriotic.

patronise (v.)
look down on, scorn, condescend, demean, humiliate
They were patronised by their superiors.

paunch (n.)
belly, pot-belly
He has a huge paunch, and he needs to lose weight.

pauper (n.)
beggar, mendicant, tramp, hobo, vagrant
His was the classic story of being pauper to prince.

pause (v.)
hesitate, interrupt, delay, hold up, discontinue, break, wait, mark time, suspend, intermit, falter, rest
He paused for her to answer.

pawn (v.)
pledge, mortgage, hypothecate, plight, deposit
I had to pawn my watch to get enough money to eat.

pay (v.)
recompense, compensate, remunerate, reward, repay, refund, reimburse
The family has to pay the bank a lot of money.

peace (n.)
serenity, tranquillity, calm, mind, quiet, harmony, amity
Everyone has their own idea of peace.

peak (n.)
top, pinnacle, crest, summit, mountain, hill
The peaks of the mountain looked unreachable.

peasant (n.)
rustic, countryman, farmer, provincial, worker
Peasants have no voice most of the times.

peculiar (adj.)
odd, strange, bizarre, weird, unusual, abnormal, anomalous, aberrant, eccentric, uncommon, outlandish,

exceptional
His is a peculiar way of doing things.

pedantic (adj.)
didactic, pedagogic, preachy, professorial, bookish, ostentatious
He has a pedantic air about him.

pedestal (n.)
foundation, base, platform, stand, substructure, mounting
The men put her on a pedestal.

pedestrian (n.)
walker, stroller, rambler, footslogger
For pedestrians, special arrangements have been made.

peevish (adj.)
irritable, touchy, fretful, waspish, petulant, querulous, short-tempered, ill-natured, bad-tempered
She's quite peevish today.

penalise (v.)
punish, discipline, fine, amerce, sentence
The law penalises criminals mercilessly.

penalty (n.)
punishment, discipline, sentence, fine, mulct
He has to pay heavy penalty for his misdemeanours.

penance (n.)
punishment, penalty, reparation, amends, atonement, self-punishment, self-mortification, regret, repentance, contrition, suffering, penitence
A year of public service was fair penance for the offence.

penchant (n.)
inclination, predisposition, tendency, affinity, liking, preference, fondness, taste
Molly has a penchant for old books.

penetration (n.)
piercing, perforation, incision, puncture, entry
The penetration of any body-part in any surgery is a matter of great care.

pensive (adj.)
thoughtful, meditative, musing, contemplative, reflective, ruminative,

brooding, serious
The scholar was in a pensive mood, when I entered the room.

penurious (adj.)
stingy, mean, penny-pinching, miserly, niggardly, parsimonious, thrifty
She is never going to change; she is as penurious as one can get.

perceptible (adj.)
discernible, observable, perceivable, noticeable, recognizable, apparent, evident, obvious, palpable, plain
The flaws in the painting are perceptible.

percolate (v.)
seep, steep, transfuse, filter, pervade, filtrate, trickle, permeate
The water percolated into the earth, reaching the roots of the plants.

perdition (n.)
damnation, hell, doom, ruin, destruction, downfall
Is every crime to be punished with perdition?

peremptory (adj.)
commanding, imperative, compelling, mandatory, irrefutable
The peremptory call of the king could not be ignored.

perennial (adj.)
lasting, persistent, incessant, uninterrupted, continual
Traffic jam has been a perennial problem with the city.

perfection (n.)
purity, flawlessness, faultlessness, sublimity, superiority, excellence, quintessence
Everyone strives for perfection in whatever they do.

perfidious (adj.)
treacherous, deceitful, traitorous, treasonable, disloyal, false, untrue, insidious, corrupt
His perfidious sister betrayed him.

performance (n.)
show, exhibition, play, act
The performances at the Best Marigold Hotel were fascinating.

perfunctory (adj.)
routine, mechanical, automatic, inattentive, indifferent, unconcerned, offhand, superficial, cursory
I do not like the perfunctory courtesy in these weddings.

peril (n.)
danger, threat, risk, jeopardy
The woman's life was in peril.

periphery (n.)
circumference, border, edge, rim, boundary, margins
The real issue has really been on the periphery.

perky (adj.)
lively, cheery, invigorated, vigorous, spirited, sprightly, animated, vivacious, bubbly
She's been quite perky since she started the new dance class.

permanence (n.)
stability, durability, fixedness, longevity, persistence, reliability
The permanence of the plan is doubtful.

permission (n.)
consent, assent, license, sanction, authorization, approval, liberty
We are still waiting for the school's permission.

perpetrate (v.)
commit, execute, perform, carry out, effectuate, accomplish, do
The crimes were perpetrated without any consideration for humanity.

perpetual (adj.)
eternal, infinite, ageless, permanent, unceasing, lasting, unvarying, unchanging, immutable
We had a perpetual desire to travel.

perplex (v.)
confuse, bewilder, puzzle, baffle, befuddle, confound, muddle, stump, nonplus, stupefy, stun
It was just a simple math problem that perplexed the man.

perquisite (n.)
consideration, emolument, bonus, bonus, dividend, gratuity, tip

quarry (n.)
prey, game, prize, object
Young girls are seen as potential quarries by men.

quash (v.)
annul, nullify, invalidate, revoke, vacate, cancel, reject, overthrow
They quashed the agreement we had earlier.

quasi- (adv).
as if, seemingly, apparently, partly, to some extent, more or less, virtually, somewhat
His role in the movie was quasi-dramatic.

queasy (adj.)
uncomfortable, uneasy, nervous, troubled, discomfited, nauseous, sick
She had a queasy feeling about going to the office after what had happened.
He felt queasy after the boat ride.

queen (n.)
sovereign, monarch, ruler, empress
The Queen had come down to see the visitors.

queer (adj.)
odd, strange, different, peculiar, uncommon, atypical, exceptional, unusual, weird, bizarre, offbeat, irregular, eccentric, absurd
His queer manner drew everyone's attention to himself.

quell (v.)
suppress, repress, subdue, quash, overcome, crush
The soldiers quelled the rebellion using violent ways.

quench (v.)
satisfy, slake, sate, surfeit, satiate, appease
Her thirst could not be quenched even after two glasses of water.

querulous (adj.)
complaining, carping, hypercritical, finicky, fussy, petulant, peevish, testy, irritable, annoyed, piqued, irascible, quarrelsome, cantankerous, fretful
His querulous attitude is not going to make him popular in the group.

query (n.)
question, inquiry, enquiry
The information desk is

made to answer all your queries.

quest (n. & v.)
search, pursuit, exploration, expedition, voyage, mission, chase, hunt
His quest was to travel the world alone. (n.)
She quested for solitude in the quiet towns of Greenland. (v.)

questionable (adj.)
doubtful, dubious, debatable, moot, disputable, suspicious, arguable, unsure
The advantages of starving oneself are questionable.

queue (n.)
line, row, string, train, retinue, chain
Cutting a queue is frowned upon everyone.

quibble (v.)
equivocate, split hairs, evade, palter
People quibbled about which painting to put in the hall.

quick (adj.)
rapid, fast, speedy, swift, expeditious, express
We made a quick run to the marketplace.

quietly (adv.)
silently, soundlessly, noiselessly, inaudibly, softly
She went quietly out of the church.

quintessence (n.)
essence, heart, core, epitome, embodiment, model, exemplar, ideal, paragon
Pablo Picasso's work for many people is the quintessence of painting.

quip (n.)
witticism, jest, joke, gibe, barb, aphorism, epigram, apothegm, pun, double entendre
He made his quips about dinner the other day.

quirk (n.)
peculiarity, caprice, eccentricity, idiosyncrasy, oddity, whim
Some quirk of fate led to their meeting again.

quit (v.)
leave, depart from, exit, desert, forsake, abandon
He is quitting the

company due to some personal problem.

quixotic (adj.)

idealistic, impractical, unrealistic, visionary, romantic, fanciful, dreamy, rash, reckless, wild

His quixotic outlook made world an easy place for him.

quizzical (adj.)

curious, queer, inquiring, questioning, puzzled

The man had a quizzical expression on his face.

quotation (n.)

quote, passage, citation, reference

Many people use quotations when they make speeches.

□

R

rabid (adj.)
unreasonable, raging, furious, violent, crazed, maniacal, infuriated, frenetic
She gets rabid on the subject of marriage.

raconteur (n.)
storyteller, anecdotist, narrator
Jessica is an amazing raconteur.

radiance (n.)
brightness, brilliance, resplendence, luminosity, dazzle, sparkle, scintillation, twinkle, glow, gleam, shine
The radiance of her face was mesmerising.

radical (adj.)
basic, fundamental, elementary, inherent, essential, cardinal, principal, primary, deep
There is a radical problem with his statement.

raillery (n.)
banter, badinage, persiflage, repartee, frivolity, joking, jesting, chaffing, teasing, ridicule
It was just some raillery that she had to face.

raise (v.)
lift, elevate, pull up, haul up
She raised her hand to answer the question.

rakish (adj.)
dashing, dapper, spruce, debonair, raffish, smart
His rakish ways made him popular amongst women.

ramble (v.)
amble, wander, stroll, saunter, walk, travel, drift, rove
Don't ramble too far as it is not safe.

ramification (n.)
consequence, result, effect, upshot, implication
The ramifications of his

decisions would be far-reaching.

rampage (n.)
agitation, recklessness, riot, tumult, fury
He went on a rampage after drinking.

rampant (adj.)
unchecked, uninhibited, unrestrained, wild, unbridled, uncontrollable
There is rampant poverty in that part of the country.

ramshackle (adj.)
dilapidated, crumbling, rickety, unsteady, decrepit, shaky, unstable, tottering, ruined
He has been living in that ramshackle house for twenty years.

rancid (adj.)
stinking, reeking, smelly, malodorous
I think that rancid smell is coming from the room.

rancour (n.)
hatred, hate, antipathy, spite, resentment, antagonism, hostility, malignity, malevolence, enmity
The rancour between them was senseless.

ransom (n.)
rescue, release, liberation
The man was held to ransom by a group of kidnappers.

rant (v.)
declaim, expatiate, orate, pontificate, trumpet, harangue
The priest ranted pompously about his priestly powers.

rapacious (adj.)
greedy, covetous, avaricious, usurious, acquisitive, predacious, ravenous, voracious, wolfish
The rapacious man took everything from the people in the bus.

rape (n. & v.)
ravishment, deflowering, violation, sexual assault
The police are not registering complaints of rape. (n.)
The man raped her at gun point. (v.)

rapport (n.)
bond, relationship, understanding
He has an amazing with rapport with the kids.

rapture (n.)
ecstasy, delight, joyfulness, exaltation, elation, thrill, enchantment, euphoria
He felt a tremendous sense of rapture on receiving the much-awaited award.

rarefied (adj.)
thin, lean, attenuated, sparse, scant
As we went in deeper, the rarefied space made seeing almost impossible.

rarity (n.)
oddity, curio, find, treasure
That ancient coin is a rarity in his collection.

rash (adj.)
impetuous, impulsive, thoughtless, foolhardy, injudicious, imprudent, careless, reckless, wild, venturesome, brash
It was a rash decision on his part to not wear a helmet while riding the motorcycle.

ratify (v.)
approve, sanction, endorse, corroborate, uphold, validate, substantiate, verify, authenticate, certify
All members in the committee ratified the policy.

rational (adj.)
sane, sound, normal, reasonable, logical, ratiocinative, clear-headed
Othello claimed to be a rational person; still he killed Desdemona.

rationale (n.)
reason, explanation, logical basis, grounds, logic, reasoning, philosophy, principle, theory
I did not understand the rationale behind his decision.

raucous (adj.)
harsh, rough, grating, discordant, dissonant, jarring, shrill, noisy, loud
A raucous shriek was heard from the bird's cage.

ravage (v.)
devastate, destruct, ruin, destroy, demolish, raze, wreck, damage, plunder, ransack
The dacoits ravaged the

village by taking almost everything.

ravenous (adj.)
hungry, famished, starving
We used to be ravenous after the swimming sessions.

ravishing (adj.)
dazzling, gorgeous, striking, charming, alluring, entrancing, captivating, bewitching, spellbinding
She seemed to be a ravishing presence in the party last night.

reach (v.)
hold out, extend, stretch, stick out, thrust out, outstretch
She reached out for his hand and he instantly held hers tightly.

react (v.)
act, behave, reciprocate, respond
She reacted in a surprisingly cool manner.

reactionary (adj. & n.)
conservative, rightist, right-wing, blimpish, traditionalist
Reactionary regimes tend to cut down on free public services. (adj.)
I can say this without a doubt that he is a reactionary. (n.)

read (v.)
peruse, scan, skim, review, study
I have to read the book again to remember it.

readily (adv.)
cheerfully, willingly, eagerly, unhesitatingly, freely, gladly, happily, agreeably, graciously
She readily accepted the offer that the company had made to her.

real (adj.)
genuine, true, actual, authentic, verified, bona fide, natural
The diamonds that Rachel wears are not real.

realistic (adj.)
practical, pragmatic, sensible, reasonable, rational, unromantic
His realistic assessment of the situation saved our lives.

realisation (n.)
understanding, comprehension,

awareness, recognition, cognizance, apprehend
He had a moment of realisation after he spoke to his father.

realm (n.)
domain, kingdom, empire, monarchy, territory, area, space, sphere
This issue cannot be accommodated within the realm of logic.

reasonable (adj.)
sensible, rational, sane, logical, judicious, wise, intelligent, thinking
She is a reasonable person to whom I can talk.

rebel (v. & n.)
revolt, mutiny, rise up, revolutionize
They are rebelling against the tyrannical regime. (v.)
He seems to be a rebel. (n.)

rebirth (n.)
renaissance, revival, renewal, reawakening, resurgence, resurrection, regeneration, reincarnation
The rebirth of arts and aesthetics was necessary for human civilisation.

rebound (v.)
spring back, bounce, recoil, ricochet
The trick hilariously rebounded.

rebuff (n.)
rejection, snub, refusal, dismissal, defeat, repudiation, slight
The rebuff he had to face embarrassed him deeply.

rebuke (v.)
scold, reproach, admonish, reprove, reprimand, chide, reprehend, berate, castigate
He rebuked her for her immodest outfit.

rebuttal (n.)
answer, reply, retort, response, rejoinder
His rebuttal of her argument was justified.

recalcitrant (adj.)
stubborn, obstinate, defiant, headstrong, ungovernable, unyielding, adamant
The recalcitrant students would be expelled from the annual function.

recall (v.)
remember, recollect, reminisce over
She liked to recall the happy memories of the past.

recede (v.)
ebb, subside, abate, withdraw, retreat
When the waters receded, the beach became visible.

recent (adj.)
latest, new, current, contemporary
This has been a recent development in the plan.

receptive (adj.)
open, hospitable, amenable, pervious, persuasible, tractable, flexible, pliant, interested, willing, responsive
I have always found Peggy receptive to suggestions on improving productivity and efficiency.

recession (n.)
set-back, slump, decline, dip, depression
The recession was a product of the crawling of the economy.

reciprocal (adj.)
mutual, exchanged, complementary, shared
People like the idea of reciprocal courtesies.

reckless (adj.)
careless, rash, incautious, heedless, injudicious, impulsive, irresponsible, negligent, unmindful
She is a reckless person and is, therefore, not reliable.

reclaim (v.)
restore, recover, rescue, redeem, salvage, retrieve
They could reclaim some of their money.

reclusive (adj.)
solitary, lone, secluded, isolated, hermitic, monastic, cloistered, sequestered
His reclusive life amazes me.

recognition (n.)
identification, detection, cognizance
Her recognition of the art forms made the visit to the museum fun.

recoil (v.)
jump, spring back, flinch, shrink
She recoiled when a lizard accidentally fell on her.

recommend (v.)
advise, suggest, advocate, propose, propound
She recommended that the décor of the hotel should be altered.

reconcile (v.)
unite, reunite, settle, placate
It looks like they are going to reconcile their differences.

recondite (adj.)
abstruse, deep, profound, incomprehensible, unfathomable, impenetrable, undecipherable
Harry's recondite idea is not going to take him far.

recount (v.)
relate, narrate, tell, recite, communicate
Vyasa recounted the epic tale of Pandavas and Kauravas to his disciples.

recourse (n.)
resort, access, availability
These people were without recourse to aid from their neighbours.

recovery (n.)
recuperation, restoration, improvement, healing, amelioration
Everyone was surprised to see her in recovery.

recreation (n.)
entertainment, amusement, enjoyment, diversion, pastime, relaxation
His idea of recreation is poles apart from yours.

rectify (v.)
correct, revise, redress, repair, improve, emend, fix, adjust
Are you going to rectify the errors in that file?

rectitude (n.)
propriety, morality, uprightness, virtue, decency, honesty, integrity, righteousness
The moral rectitude that she has is missing from this generation.

recur (v.)
return, reoccur, repeat
The problem recurred after a few months only.

redolent (adj.)
fragrant, aromatic, perfumed, scented
The hotel room was redolent with the smell of potpourri.

redundant (adj.)
superfluous, unnecessary, surplus, inessential, unneeded
She made a redundant statement in the courtroom.

refine (v.)
purify, cleanse, clear, clarify, decontaminate, polish, elevate, civilise
She refined the person that he was.

reflective (adj.)
thoughtful, pensive, contemplative, musing, meditative, cogitative, ruminating, deliberative, pondering
I saw him in a reflective mood the other day.

reform (v. & n.)
improve, meliorate, emend, mend, repair, fix, remedy, rehabilitate, remodel, refashion
They are planning to reform the educational system. (v.)
The reforms in education are much-needed. (n.)

refuge (n.)
sanctuary, shelter, haven, protection, cover, retreat, harbour, bolt-hole, hideaway
He sought refuge under a tree in the rain.

refusal (n.)
denial, rejection, disapproval
Their refusal to the proposal was not expected.

regal (adj.)
royal, majestic, imperial, stately, splendid, magnificent, grand, resplendent
The regal palace left them awestruck.

regime (n.)
regimen, reign, government, rule, administration, leadership, management, system
The old regime was better than this one.

regretful (adj.)
rueful, mournful, repentant, guilty, sorrowful, remorseful, apologetic, penitent
She was regretful about the behaviour of her husband in public.

regularity (n.)
consistency, constancy, uniformity, evenness,

orderliness, stability
The regularity of Professor Meera is laudable.

regulate (v.)
adjust, modify, modulate, control, govern, organise, maintain
It is hard to regulate the behaviour of perverse people.

rehearse (v.)
practise, exercise, study
Let's rehearse that scene for the show.

reiterate (v.)
repeat, restate, iterate, recapitulate
I have reiterated the instructions to the students.

rejection (n.)
refusal, denial, repudiation, dismissal, spurning
The rejection of his overtures left him heart-broken.

rejoice (v.)
delight, exult, glory, celebrate
They rejoiced after winning the match.

rejuvenate (v.)
restore, refresh, reinvigorate, revitalise, renew, reanimate, regenerate, recharge
The vacation rejuvenated the family.

relentless (adj.)
unyielding, inflexible, unbending, unmoving, rigid, determined, undeviating, intractable, persevering, unsparing, ruthless
His relentless pursuit of her paid off.

relevance (n.)
appropriateness, aptness, pertinence, significance, suitability, applicability
The relevance of his statement is questionable.

reliable (adj.)
dependable, trustworthy, credible, believable, responsible
I am not sure that Joey is a reliable person.

religious (adj.)
devout, pious, holy
Cassie has a religious temperament.

relish (n. & v.)
enjoyment, pleasure,

delight, eagerness, taste, liking, appreciation, fondness
My husband ate the dish with great relish. (n.)
I relish the fact that the salary would increase. (v.)

reluctant (adj.)
unwilling, disinclined, averse, hesitant, unenthusiastic, indisposed, opposed
Hannah was reluctant to let go of her child.

remarkable (adj.)
extraordinary, unusual, exceptional, noteworthy, incredible, unbelievable, impressive, phenomenal
Marc won everyone's hearts with his remarkable talent of making scrumptious food.

reminisce (v.)
remember, recollect
People reminisce about things of the past.

remorse (n.)
regret, repentance, ruefulness, sorrow, woe, humiliation, embarrassment, guilt, self-reproach
She felt remorse about doing injustice to her sister.

renounce (v.)
forsake, forswear, surrender, forgo
She renounced the comforts of her home for the sake of love.

renowned (adj.)
famed, celebrated, distinguished, acclaimed, eminent, notable, illustrious
She was one of the most renowned painters in the country.

repartee (n.)
banter, badinage, persiflage, wordplay, raillery
She conversed with a hint of repartee.

repercussion (n.)
reaction, response, effect, outcome, consequence, reverberation, result, aftermath, after-effect, upshot, fallout, backlash, echo
The flood was repercussion of cutting trees and soil erosion.

repetitive (adj.)
iterative, repetitious,

monotonous, repeated, redundant, humdrum, unceasing, recurrent
The repetitive nature of our lives sometimes becomes unbearable.

repose (n.)
calm, respite, tranquillity, quiet, restfulness, peace
They were searching for repose in the mountains.

representative (adj.)
symbolic, typical, characteristic, emblematic, archetypal, evocative, illustrative
This sample is representative of the final product.

repress (v.)
suppress, curb, stifle, control, contain, restrain, constrain, quell, subdue, hamper
He repressed her in many ways, and, that is why, she never speaks.

reprimand (n. & v.)
scolding, reproof, rebuke, admonition, upbraiding, castigation, remonstrance, reprehension, chiding
The boy received a severe reprimand for breaking the glass pane. (n.)
Holly was reprimanded for her conduct in the assembly. (v.)

reprisal (n.)
retaliation, revenge, retribution, requital, vengeance, repayment, vindication
They shot women and children in reprisal.

reprobate (adj.)
unprincipled, immoral, depraved, despicable, dissolute, low, debased, degenerate, profligate
His reprobate way was disturbing for his colleagues.

repudiate (v.)
reject, scorn, renounce, retract, rescind, forswear, forgo, disown
King Dushyanta repudiated Sakuntala's claim of wifehood in his court.

reputable (adj.)
respectable, honourable, respected, trustworthy
Charlie is one of the most reputable teachers in the university.

request (v. & n.)
ask for, seek, plead,

requisition, demand, solicit, entreat, beseech
Watson requested to be excused from the meeting. (v.)
I have a request to make regarding room cleaning. (n.)

requirement (n.)
requisite, demand, precondition, condition, demand, necessity
Sam's requirement of a clean is not a huge one.

rescue (v. & n.)
save, deliver, liberate, release
All the denizens were rescued before the tsunami could hit the city. (v.)
A rescue mission is going to be conducted by the team. (n.)

research (n. & v.)
investigation, exploration, delving, scrutinisation, examination, inspection, probing, analysis
Julie's research went off-track, as she chose a topic that did not pertain to her domain. (n.)
She researched about the species about the numerous species of fish in that particular water-body. (v.)

resemblance (n.)
likeness, similarity, similitude, congruity, equivalence, semblance, alikeness
The resemblance is between the two siblings is uncanny.

resentful (adj.)
embittered, bitter, acrimonious, spiteful, begrudging, displeased, disgruntled
She is resentful but no one knows the reason for that.

reserved (adj.)
reticent, restrained, silent, taciturn, uncommunicative, unforthcoming, undemonstrative, standoffish, unsocial, distant, remote, detached, withdrawn, guarded
He is peculiarly reserved in some matters.

residence (n.)
abode, home, domicile, dwelling, place, house,

habitation
We were waiting for her outside her residence.

residual (adj.)
remaining, leftover, surplus, spare
The residual matter at the bottom of the flask has to be removed.

resignation (n.)
abandonment, abdication, renunciation, forgoing, relinquishment
Mary submitted her resignation last evening itself.

resilience (n.)
rebound, recoil, bounce, elasticity, springiness, flexibility
One of the qualities of youth is resilience.

resistance (n.)
opposition, defiance, obstruction, intransigence, rebelliousness, recalcitrance
India employed different strategies of resistance for independence.

resolute (adj.)
resolved, determined, steadfast, firm, staunch, dauntless, persevering, persistent, pertinacious, tenacious
His resolute manner made everything possible.

resonant (adj.)
vibrant, resounding, reverberant, pulsating, ringing
The resonant sound of the horn became intolerable.

resourceful (adj.)
ingenious, inventive, imaginative, clever, creative, skilful, smart
Being resourceful is important for survival.

restitution (n.)
amends, compensation, redress, recompense, reparation, requital
Restitution is what the victims rightfully deserve.

restless (adj.)
restive, uneasy, edgy, fidgety, nervous, agitated, antsy
They were becoming restless by the end of the movie.

restraint (n.)
control, check, curb,

It is traditional to provide each member in the company a Diwali bonus as a perquisite.

persecution (n.)
oppression, subjugation, maltreatment, abuse, outrage, victimization, tyranny, affliction, punishment
People have suffered persecution because of the difference of faith.

perseverance (n.)
steadfastness, determination, stamina, tirelessness, patience, diligence, devotion, tenacity
Perseverance is a quality needed for success.

persist (v.)
insist (on), strive, toil
She persists about the figure that she sees in the hallway.

persona (n.)
face, exterior, role, part, character, identity, self, personality
I like her outdoorsy persona.

personal (adj.)
individual, physical, actual, live
The politician is going to make a personal appearance.

perspective (n.)
viewpoint, standpoint, position
His perspective is different from others.

perspiration (n.)
sweat
The perspiration on his forehead could not be missed.

persuade (v.)
urge, induce, influence, sway, press
The strange man persuaded him to lie.

pertinent (adj.)
appropriate, fitting, suitable, apt, relevant, germane
Your comments should be pertinent to the topic.

perturb (v.)
upset, disturb, fluster, unsettle, disconcert, vex, confuse
Clark became quite perturbed when he heard about the accident.

perusal (n.)
reading, scrutiny, examination, study,

inspection
I saw nothing problematic in my perusal of the book.

perverse (adj.)
wrong, awry, wayward, irregular
It was most perverse of her to break the promise.

pessimistic (n.)
gloomy, negative, hopeless, despondent, defeatist, cynical, bleak
He is quite pessimistic about everything new.

pester (v.)
annoy, nag, irritate, irk, bother, badger, vex, hector, pique
The men were pestering him to drink.

petite (adj.)
delicate, dainty, small, little, slight, tiny
She is too petite for him.

petrify (v.)
frighten, scare, horrify, terrify, paralyse, numb, benumb
I was petrified by the sound outside my room.

petty (adj.)
trivial, paltry, minor, inferior, trifling, puny, inconsequential, unimportant
This bunch has been jailed only for petty crimes.

phantom (n.)
apparition, spectre, ghost, spirit, phantasm, shade, revenant, vision
The phantom of the opera remained a mystery for a long time.

phase (n.)
stage, period, development
Their relationship is just going through a phase.

phenomenal (adj.)
outstanding, remarkable, exceptional, extraordinary, unusual, rare, incredible, marvellous, amazing, astonishing, staggering, stunning, fantastic
She had a phenomenal presence tonight.

phenomenon (n.)
event, happening, occurrence, incident, experience
The phenomenon of rain is known to everyone.

philanderer (n.)
flirt, gallant, rake, Casanova
Her husband is such a philanderer, and she is completely unaware about it.

philanthropist (n.)
contributor, donor, benefactor, humanitarian, altruist
The famous actor is also a philanthropist, as he always helps the needy.

philosophical (adj.)
abstract, learned, scholarly, erudite
Michael has a philosophical temperament.

phlegmatic (adj.)
unemotional, unenthusiastic, apathetic, unfeeling, uncaring, cold, stolid, unaffected, indifferent, uninterested, passive
Saul has a phlegmatic disposition in general.

phobia (n.)
fear, horror, terror, dread, hatred, revulsion, dislike, qualm, apprehension
There are several kinds of phobias in this world.

phoney (adj.)
unreal, fake, artificial, factitious, false, fraudulent, bogus, counterfeit, sham, pretended, dissimulating
He trapped everyone into his phoney schemes by sugar-coating the benefits.

photograph (n.)
napshot, print, picture, slide, photo, snap
Shaliya has taken some amazing nature photographs.

physical (adj.)
bodily, corporeal, corporal, fleshly, carnal, mortal, earthly
Raima has the physical strength to lift this bag of flour.

pictorial (adj.)
graphic, picturesque, vivid, telling, striking, expressive, plain, clear
The poet gave us a pictorial description of the scene.

piecemeal (adv.)
piece by piece, little by little, inch by inch, bit by bit, gradually, by degrees, slowly, in bits and pieces, sporadically

The government thought that the drive should be carried out at once and not be as piecemeal over the next six months.

pierce (v.)
stab, puncture, penetrate, thrust into, lance, spear, skewer
The horrendous news pierced her heart.

piety (n.)
devotion, devotedness, respect, deference, dedication, dutifulness, religiosity, reverence
In the spirit of piety, he visited the deprived in the charitable home regularly.

pilfer (v.)
steal, rob, plunder, thieve, filch, embezzle, misappropriate, purloin
The bank is known for pilfering the funds.

pilgrimage (n.)
holy expedition, crusade, journey, trek, voyage, tour, trip
Muslims believe in the idea of a pilgrimage.

pillage (v.)
plunder, raid, ravage, despoil, rob, loot, ransack, maraud, vandalize, ruin, demolish, raze, strip
The dacoits pillaged every city they went to.

pinnacle (n.)
top, peak, apex, acme, summit, zenith, maximum, tip, cap, crest
Being elected principal was the pinnacle of Martha career.

pioneer (n.)
pathfinder, trail-blazer, ground-breaker, forerunner, innovator, leader, trend-setter
Graham Bell was a pioneer in the development of telephone.

pious (adj.)
devout, religious, reverential, dutiful, godly, spiritual, moral, virtuous, saintly, holy, angelic
A pious person prays every day.

piteous (adj.)
pathetic, miserable, distressing, grievous, sad, doleful, tearful, lamentable, deplorable, rueful

We heard the piteous crying of the hungry children.

pity (n.)
sympathy, compassion, tenderness
Everyone had pity for the poor state of Truman.

plagiarism (n.)
piracy, pirating, theft, purloining, stealing, copying, thievery, imitation
We discourage plagiarism in this institution.

plague (n.)
scourge, epidemic, pestilence, affliction, pandemic, evil, bane, blight, visitation
The city was suffering from the plague of mosquitoes.

platonic (adj.)
non-physical, asexual, dispassionate, spiritual, ideal, intellectual
Their relationship has always been purely platonic.

platter (n.)
server, tray, plate, dish
There are platters of fresh fruit in the hall.

plausible (adj.)
likely, believable, reasonable, tenable, conceivable, admissible, sensible, logical, acceptable
It is not plausible to change hotel rooms every night.

play (v.)
amusement, frolic, cavort, gambol, caper, sport, carouse
We were playing outside the house.

player (n.)
contestant, participant, competitor, contender, athlete, sportsperson
The players of the opposition are more astute.

plea (n.)
request, entreaty, appeal, petition, cry, solicitation
His pleas were genuine, and he needs help.

pleasant (adj.)
pleasing, good, lovely, attractive, enjoyable, delightful, charming, agreeable
The house is a combination of pleasant hues and smells.

pleasure (n.)
enjoyment, happiness, delight, joy, satisfaction, contentment, gratification, recreation, amusement, entertainment
They take great pleasure in receiving their guests.

plebeian (adj.)
proletarian, working-class, lower-class, lowly, common, humble, peasantry
He has plebian interests, and is not to be invited in the gathering.

pledge (n.)
promise, oath, vow, word, covenant
We pledge to bring everyone back from the fire.

plentiful (adj.)
ample, abundant, copious, lavish, plenteous, bountiful, generous
They had plentiful food supply in that part of the town.

pliable (adj.)
flexible, pliant, elastic, malleable, workable, bendable, ductile
Plastic and glass is pliable in molten form.

plight (n.)
condition, state, circumstances, situation, predicament
We empathize with the plight of displaced people.

plot (n.)
scheme, plan, intrigue, machination, conspiracy
Their plot to kill him did not succeed.

plunge (v.)
descend, drop, plummet, dive, nosedive, fall
They plunged into the sea to swim.

plush (adj.)
luxurious, posh, palatial, lavish, rich, opulent, regal, elegant
His plush home was a proof of his class.

poem (n.)
verse, lyric, rhyme, song, ode
The book contains poems by amateurs.

poetic (adj.)
poetical, metrical, musical, melodic

His poetic vision was an eye-opener for me.

poignant (adj.)
distressing, grievous, painful, woeful, pitiable, moving, touching
The poignant portrayal of his story was remarkable.

pointless (adj.)
purposeless, aimless, meaningless, ineffectual, futile, unproductive, fruitless, senseless, inane, preposterous, empty
The students made pointless comments in the class.

poise (n.)
composure, control, dignity, equanimity, staidness, reserve, calmness
She remained poise in the face of adversity.

poison (n.)
toxin, venom
She kills insects using poison.

polish (v.)
shine, brighten, burnish, buff, smoothen, gloss
He polished his shoes obsessively.

polite (adj.)
civil, respectful, mannerly, courteous
His was a polite response to her question.

pollution (n.)
contamination, adulteration, corruption, befouling, soiling, spoiling, staining
Pollution, in its many forms, is a common evil.

pomp (n.)
glory, grandeur, magnificence, splendour, extravaganza, ceremony, spectacle
The pomp of the Roman courts was unmatchable.

popular (adj.)
favoured, accepted, approved, fashionable, stylish, celebrated, renowned, famous
Facebook is a popular virtual platform these days.

portable (adj.)
transportable, manageable, carriable, handy
Is this washing machine portable?

portentous (adj.)
ominous, threatening,

sinister, alarming, menacing, foreboding, ill-omened, inauspicious, unfavourable, ill-fated
The most portentous news was revealed at the very end.

portrait (n.)
picture, image, rendering, representation, description, profile, sketch
He is famous for making awe-inspiring portraits.

poseur (n.)
posturer, pretender, impostor, masquerader, dissembler, fraud
He shows himself to be a connoisseur, but he is just a poseur.

posit (v.)
postulate, hypothesise, propound, propose, pose
The alien world posits to be a grave threat to the human world.

positive (adj.)
sure, certain, definite, unequivocal, absolute, unqualified, unquestionable, uncontested, undeniable
The people have positive proof that the stranger was the thief.

possess (v.)
have, own
They possessed great riches in their prime.

possibility (n.)
chance, odds, prospect, feasibility, plausibility, likelihood
I do see the possibility of us meeting again.

postpone (v.)
delay, adjourn, defer, suspend
We have to postpone this meeting.

potent (adj.)
powerful, strong, mighty, vigorous, formidable, influential
Snake venom could be potent poison.

poverty (n.)
want, penury, destitution, pauperism, neediness, deprivation
They lived in poverty during childhood.

practical (adj.)
pragmatic, functional, realistic, reasonable
It was a practical decision to make.

praise (n.)
acclaim, approbation, applause, tribute, accolade, compliments
Carol received praise for her projects.

prank (n.)
trick, joke, frolic, escapade, antic, jest
They used pranks to make people laugh.

pray (v.)
beseech, ask, entreat, implore, request, supplicate
I pray you to God to thank him for all he has given me.

precarious (adj.)
uncertain, unreliable, risky, hazardous, unpredictable, tricky, delicate
If sales continue to drop, the company will be in precarious condition.

precaution (n.)
provision, safeguard, insurance, protection
We have to take precautions, in case there is a fire.

precept (n.)
rule, guide, principle, guideline, dictate, code, law, commandment, instruction, directive
The precepts of life are learned the hard way.

precision (n.)
correctness, exactness, exactitude, preciseness, accuracy
His precision in surgery is exceptional.

precocious (adj.)
advanced, mature, early, intelligent, smart
There are a few precocious children in the world.

preconceived (adj.)
predisposed, prejudged, predetermined, prejudiced
People have numerous preconceived notions about other people.

precursor (n.)
harbinger, herald, vanguard, forerunner
The glistening effect on the western horizon is the precursor of another night.

predestination (n.)
destiny, fortune, fate, foreordination, preordain
The way we ran into

each other was plain predestination.

predicament (n.)
dilemma, quandary, situation, state, condition, crisis
My absurd predicament was a result of non-thinking.

prediction (n.)
forecast, prophecy, augury, prognosis
Most of her predictions come true.

prejudice (n.)
partiality, preconception, prejudgment, bias, leaning, predisposition, predilection
Samantha's mother's prejudice is clearly visible in her treatment of her kids.

premeditated (adj.)
planned, conscious, intentional, deliberate, studied, preplanned, calculated, preconceived
The robbery was definitely premeditated, as it was carried out with such precision.

preposterous (adj.)
absurd, ridiculous, ludicrous, asinine, foolish, senseless, irrational, nonsensical, fatuous, mindless, insane
His preposterous suggestion could not have been entertained.

prerequisite (adj.)
essential, necessary, imperative, indispensable, obligatory, required
To sit for the entrance, it is a prerequisite requirement to carry your admit card.

prerogative (n.)
privilege, right, liberty, power, advantage
It is your prerogative to choose the front or back row seats in the theatre.

presentable (adj.)
fitting, suitable, acceptable, passable, tolerable, admissible
She did not seem presentable after the hullabaloo before the wedding ceremony.

preservation (n.)
upkeep, maintenance, care, conservation
The preservation of wildlife is our motto at the moment.

prestige (n.)
status, reputation, stature, importance, significance, eminence, esteem, repute
Ross's prestige was his biggest concern; he did not want to compromise with that.

presumptuous (adj.)
arrogant, prideful, audacious, bold, impertinent, insolent, brash, overconfident, presuming
Some people are presumptuous, and nobody can change that about them.

pretence (n.)
show, facade, appearance, hypocrisy, faking, feigning, humbuggery, artifice
The amicable ways of the man was sheer pretence.

pretext (n.)
excuse, camouflage, disguise, cover, veil, cloak
She called him over to her house under the pretext of charity.

previous (adj.)
former, prior, past, earlier, foregoing, erstwhile, preceding
The previous account of the murder seems believable.

prey (n.)
kill, objective, target
The lion kept a sharp eye on its prey.

pride (n.)
honour, self-esteem, self-respect, dignity
It is a matter of great pride for the country to see its soldiers fighting bravely for the national cause.

priggish (adj.)
conservative, prim, demure, prudish, puristic, pedantic, conformist, strict, fastidious, fussy
The neighbours who have just moved in seem priggish.

primitive (adj.)
original, aboriginal, earliest, primordial, primaeval
Their primitive ways are different from the modern ones.

principle (n.)
truth, precept, tenet, law,

rule, doctrine, teaching, axiom, maxim, truism
We had told you to follow all the principles.

priority (n.)
precedency, primacy, preference
One has to set one's priorities right.

pristine (adj.)
clean, pure
The pristine quality of the diamond made it irresistible.

privation (n.)
need, want, deprivation, poverty, penury, destitution, pauperism
The family has been living in a state of privation for a year.

probe (v.)
explore, examine, scrutinize, investigate, look into, study, dig into
They probed him thoroughly during the investigation.

problematic (adj.)
difficult, uncertain, questioned, doubted, disputable, moot, controversial
He found her holding Sam's hand extremely problematic.

procession (n.)
parade, march, cavalcade, motorcade
A noisy procession was going outside the house.

proclamation (n.)
announcement, advertisement, declaration, publication, promulgation, statement
A proclamation is required to sort this matter.

procrastinate (v.)
temporize, evade, delay, stall, postpone, defer
It is human nature to procrastinate tasks at hand.

prodigal (adj.)
wasteful, extravagant, spendthrift, lavish, excessive, profligate, squandering, intemperate, wanton
If the wedding were less prodigal, it would be possible to save some money.

prodigy (n.)
genius, wonder child

He was a prodigy at the age of four and went on to become a great singer.

profane (adj.)
irreverent, sacrilegious, blasphemous, irreligious, heathen, godless, sinful
His profane act had to be dismissed.

profess (v.)
assert, claim, aver, state, declare, say, present, proffer, pronounce
She professed the medicinal use of neem.

proficiency (n.)
facility, talent, adeptness, expertise, skilfulness, dexterity, capability, competency
They displayed proficiency in the art of painting.

profitable (adj.)
beneficial, productive, lucrative, fruitful, gainful, remunerative, rewarding
This business does not seem to be profitable.

profligate (adj.)
debauched, immoral, unprincipled, sinful, evil, wicked, degenerate, depraved, corrupt, lecherous, lascivious, perverted
Some kings lived a profligate life.

profound (adj.)
deep, unfathomable, abstruse, intricate, knotty, inscrutable
Watching *The Godfather* was a profound experience.

prognosticate (v.)
predict, foretell, prophesy, forecast, presage, divine, forebode
The prophet prognosticated the apocalypse that was to come.

prohibition (n.)
forbiddance, bar, banning, disallowance, interdiction, outlawing, debarment
The prohibition on smoking has many supporters.

proliferate (v.)
grow, increase, burgeon, multiply, breed, reproduce
Food-trucks are proliferating in every part of the city.

promiscuous (adj.)
loose, unchaste, wanton, wild, uninhibited, unrestrained, libertine, licentious, unfaithful
One cannot trust anyone who has promiscuous ways.

prompt (adj.)
quick, immediate, instantaneous, rapid, fast, swift, speedy, timely, instant, brisk
I thanked the customer service for their prompt response.

proof (n.)
evidence, verification, corroboration, confirmation, validation, authentication, certification, testimony
We are looking for some proof to find the murderer.

propitiatory (adj.)
conciliatory, pacifying, appeasing, expiatory, placatory
To end the fight, a propitiatory hand has to be held out by one of the factions.

proponent (n.)
proposer, promoter, supporter, upholder, subscriber, patron, espouser, adherent, enthusiast, champion, advocate, exponent, spokesperson
She is a staunch proponent of the feminist movement.

prosaic (adj.)
dull, banal, commonplace, hackneyed, routine, everyday, ordinary, common, trite, jejune, boring, unimaginative, humdrum, monotonous
His prosaic manner was a letdown for her.

protagonist (n.)
hero, heroine, lead
There were no protagonists in the text.

provocation (n.)
grounds, reason, cause, instigation, incitement, stimulus, motivation, inducement
The murder was a direct result of provocation.

prudence (n.)
discretion, judgment, awareness, wariness, caution, circumspection
Prudence is necessary in dangerous situations.

pry (v.)
investigate, examine, peek, enquire
They were prying about the missing jewellery.

pseudonym (n.)
alias, pen-name, stage name, incognito
George Eliot was the pseudonym of Mary Ann Evans.

psychological (adj.)
mental, intellectual, cerebral, subjective
She has psychological problems because of her loss.

puerile (adj.)
childish, immature, infantile, juvenile, silly, asinine, trivial, ridiculous, shallow
He needs to give up his puerile ways and become serious.

pun (n.)
quip, witticism, double entendre
He is known for his talent for puns.

punishment (n.)
chastisement, castigation, disciplining, chastening, rebuke, admonishment
The punishment in his case was not appropriate.

pure (adj.)
unmixed, unadulterated, unalloyed, sterling, genuine
Pure gold is the most expensive.

purgative (adj.)
laxative, cathartic, diuretic
The purgative effects of writing are underestimated.

pursuit (n.)
pursuing, chasing, following, hunt, tracing, trailing, tracking
His pursuit of her was bound to fail.

puzzle (v.)
baffle, bewilder, confuse, confound, flummox, perplex, nonplus, stump
I am absolutely puzzled by what you said.

□

quaint (adj.)
curious, odd, strange, peculiar, unusual, uncommon, unorthodox, offbeat
The quaint decorations at her house explain a lot about her taste.

quake (v.)
tremble, shake, quiver, shudder, vibrate
The people quaked with fear looking at the approaching flood.

qualified (adj.)
able, capable, competent, fitted, equipped, trained, proficient, talented, adept, skilled, experienced
She is completely qualified to become a doctor.

quality (n.)
property, attribute, characteristic, mark, trait
Sherlock possesses all the qualities of becoming a painter.

qualm (n.)
second thought, doubt, hesitation, scruple, compunction, disinclination, concern
Sarah had qualms about giving money to that institution.

quandary (n.)
dilemma, difficulty, uncertainty, doubt, skepticism
I was in a quandary about whether to sell the house or not.

quantity (n.)
amount, extent, volume
The quantity of food is limited here.

quarrel (n. & v.)
dispute, argument, disagreement, discord, contention, squabble, altercation, scuffle, feud, fight, brawl
I have no quarrel with my lawyer. (n.)
They quarrelled with each other over dresses. (v.)

restriction, constraint, limitation, curtailment, ban, bound
They have put up a restraint on swimming after 6 pm.

resurgence (n.)
renaissance, renascence, rebirth, revival, reawakening, restoration, renewal, resurrection, regeneration
There has been a resurgence of old-fashioned ways.

retribution (n.)
vengeance, revenge, reprisal, retaliation, punishment, justice
His retribution was not justified.

retrospect (n.)
hindsight, reconsideration, review, remembering, recollection
In retrospect, I think we did the right thing by bringing her back.

reveal (v.)
expose, display, divulge, disclose, show
They revealed the details of the mission.

revelry (n.)
merry-making, fun, carousing, gaiety, festivity, jollity, mirth, celebration
The revelry seemed never-ending to me.

reverie (n.)
day-dream, fantasy
She seems to be deep in a reverie.

ribaldry (n.)
vulgarity, immodesty, indecency, bawdiness, wantonness, raciness, lustfulness, rakishness, lasciviousness
The ribaldry in some of children stories is alarming.

richly (adv.)
sumptuously, lavishly, luxuriously, splendidly, elaborately, exquisitely, elegantly
The house was richly decorated with artifacts.

rickety (adj.)
wobbly, unsteady, decrepit, shaky, tottering, ramshackle, flimsy, frail, dilapidated
The rickety chair would collapse at any moment.

ridicule (n. & v.)
deriding, jeering, taunting, mockery
She had to face ridicule because of what she did. (n.)
They ridiculed all the members of the committee. (v.)

rift (n.)
separation, break, split, schism, gulf, gap, conflict, disruption, breach, division
The rift between them became wider after the second incident.

righteous (adj.)
moral, just, virtuous, upstanding, upright, ethical, fair
She was a righteous person, who never did anyone any wrong.

riotous (adj.)
tumultuous, unrestrained, wild, noisy, uncontrolled, chaotic, disorderly, lawless, turbulent
The headmaster warned that he would not tolerate such riotous.

rite (n.)
ceremony, ritual, ceremonial, observance, formality, custom, practice, solemnity
The marriage rites is not treated likely.

rivalry (n.)
competition, contention, dispute, feud
Their rivalry of many years is nonsensical.

riveting (adj.)
spellbinding, engrossing, hypnotizing, transfixing, fascinating, enthralling, captivating
Their performance was absolutely riveting.

romantic (adj.)
imaginary, fictional, ideal, idealised, fantasised, fanciful
Their romantic relationship despite all the problems survived.

rouse (v.)
arouse, call, awaken, arise
I was roused from deep sleep due to the noise outside my room.

rover (n.)
wanderer, traveller, nomad, wayfarer, vagabond, vagrant
He can be called a rover,

as he does not believe in settling down.

rudimentary (adj.)
basic, essential, elementary, fundamental, primary, introductory, formative, initial
I was shocked to learn that she did not possess even a rudimentary knowledge of English.

rugged (adj.)
rough, uneven, broken, stony, rocky
The rugged landscape of the mountains made the journey uneasy.

ruin (n. & v.)
downfall, destruction, devastation, havoc, breakdown, collapse, disintegration, decay, undoing
She brought ruin upon the family. (n.)
They ruined everything that she cared for. (v.)

rupture (n. & v.)
break, rift, split, fissure, fracture, breaking, splitting, breach, severance
The rupture between the two friends was caused by him. (n.)
The crime ruptured the peace of a small town. (v)

rural (adj.)
country, pastoral, sylvan, bucolic, rustic, agrarian

ruse (n.)
trick, device, deception, maneuver, pretext, stratagem, ploy
Many ruses are employed in *The Mahabharata.*

ruthless (adj.)
pitiless, cruel, unsympathetic, merciless, harsh, fierce, remorseless, unfeeling, heartless, brutal
Criminals are thought to be ruthless.

□

S

sabotage (n. & v.)
destruction, damage, wrecking, impairment
The sabotage caused to the mission could not be repaired. (n.)
He sabotaged the mission for personal reasons. (v.)

sacred (adj.)
consecrated, hallowed, holy, blessed, sanctified, revered, venerable
Every religion has a sacred place.

sacrilege (n.)
desecration, profanation, debasement, violation, defilement, befouling, contamination
They committed a sacrilege when they entered the place without permission.

sadistic (adj.)
cruel, monstrous, brutish, beastly
People have the propensity to be sadistic at times.

safety (n.)
protection, aegis, cover, shelter, security, refuge
They ran to the safety of their house after the accident.

sage (adj. & n.)
wise, sagacious, prudent, sensible, intelligent, discerning, reasonable, logical
The man gave me some sage advice about life. (adj.)
The sage told me things that wouldn't forget. (n.)

salvage (v.)
save, recover, rescue, redeem, retrieve, reclaim
They were not able to salvage anything after the earthquake.

sanctimonious (adj.)
hypocritical, self-righteous, canting, pietistic
His sanctimonious talk is not going to lead him anywhere.

sanction (n.)
confirmation, ratification, authorization, legitimatisation, validation, licence, certification, approval, permission
He is waiting for the sanction of the other family members.

sang-froid (n.)
composure, poise, imperturbability, indifference
She kept her sang-froid in the face of adversity.

sanguine (adj.)
optimistic, rosy, confident, hopeful, expectant, enthusiastic
He took a sanguine view of the way things were then.

sarcastic (adj.)
scornful, contumelious, derisive, acrimonious, acerbic, acidic, acrid, aspersive, ironic, mocking, scathing, caustic
Her sarcastic remarks hurt me sometimes.

satanic (adj.)
diabolic, fiendish, devilish, demonic, infernal, hellish, infernal, godless, impious, unholy, sinister
His satanic practices were censured in the society.

satiate (v.)
stuff, gorge, overfill, glut, saturate
The guests were completely satiated with food.

satirize (v.)
lampoon, parody, caricature, travesty, ridicule, deride
Some moviemakers satirise the works of others.

satisfaction (n.)
gratification, comfort, fulfilment, contentment, delight, joy, enjoyment, pleasure, happiness
The satisfaction that she derived out of feeding poor kids was immense.

saunter (v.)
walk, stroll, amble, meander, wander
He sauntered over here looking for food.

saviour (n.)
rescuer, salvation, Samaritan, liberator, redeemer, deliverer, emancipator, champion
He was the saviour of

those people who were in desperate need.

savoury (adj.)
palatable, delicious, delectable, tasty, appetising, flavourful, luscious
The savoury dishes were finished soon.

scandal (n.)
shame, disgrace, embarrassment, sin, outrage
The scandal about blood diamonds is now exposed.

scarcity (n.)
lack, want, need, paucity, dearth, shortage, inadequateness
The scarcity of water is a grave issue in many countries.

scathing (adj.)
searing, incisive, cutting, virulent, vitriolic, burning, fierce
The scathing attack of the movie critics was demoralising for the director.

scatter (v.)
spread, diffuse, strew, circulate, distribute, disseminate
They scattered the seeds for growing crops.

sceptic (n.)
doubter, questioner, disbeliever, agnostic, scoffer, cynic
He has always been a sceptic.

scheming (adj.)
conniving, plotting, crafty, cunning, wily, calculating, tricky, slippery, duplicitous, deceitful
Her scheming manners are to be dealt with carefully.

scholar (n.)
academic, professor, teacher, pedagogue, expert, pundit, savant, intellectual
There are many scholars in the university.

scintillating (adj.)
sparkling, dazzling, gleaming, glittering, twinkling, shimmering, glistening, shining, radiant
Her scintillating diamond takes my breath away.

scold (v.)
reprimand, chide, reprove, criticize, censure, rebuke, berate, castigate

The parents scolded their children for breaking the furniture.

scorching (adj.)
hot, torrid, searing, parching, shrivelling, tropical, hellish, sizzling, broiling, boiling, sweltering
The scorching summers can be deadly for some people.

scorn (n. & v.)
contumely, contempt, disdain, deprecation
His actions were met with scorn. (n.)
His actions were scorned at by others. (v.)

scrawny (adj.)
bony, skinny, haggard, lean, scraggy, gaunt, angular, emaciated
I am worried about her scrawny brother.

scribe (n.)
copyist, transcriber, writer
Lord Ganesha served as a scribe for Vyasa.

scruple (n.)
compunction, qualm, reluctance, misgiving, hesitation
Morrison is a man without any scruples.

scrupulous (adj.)
careful, cautious, meticulous, exacting, precise, strict, rigorous, fastidious, painstaking
Cathy has always been scrupulous about her things.

scrutinize (v.)
examine, analyse, investigate, probe, study, inspect
They have scrutinized the photographs of the crime scene carefully.

scurvy (adj.)
low, miserable, contemptible, vile, base, despicable, rotten, ignoble, dishonourable
His scurvy activities were reported by the people in the neighbourhood.

seasoned (adj.)
experienced, trained, practised, habituated, established, veteran
He is a seasoned performer in the company.

secluded (adj.)
private, isolated, lonely, cloistered, sequestered, solitary
She is interested in a secluded existence.

secrecy (n.)
mystery, concealment, confidentiality, stealth, surreptitiousness, privacy, covertness, clandestineness
There is too much secrecy around the new mission.

sectarian (adj.)
cultist, cultish, clannish, partisan, dogmatic, factional
Their sectarian existence makes them antisocial.

secular (adj.)
worldly, terrestrial, mundane, temporal
Indian nation state is secular.

sedate (adj.)
composed, serene, peaceful, calm, tranquil, cool, collected, even-tempered, detached, imperturbable, unruffled, undisturbed, unperturbed, controlled, placid, grave, serious, sober, solemn
She remained sedate amidst all chaos.

sedentary (adj.)
seated, sitting, stationary, fixed, immobile, unmoving, housebound
She leads a sedentary lifestyle which can be harmful in the long run.

seductive (adj.)
alluring, attractive, tempting, tantalising, entrancing, bewitching, provocative
She had a seductive charm around her.

segregation (n.)
separation, segmentation, partition, isolation, sequestration, compartmentalisation, ostracism
The segregation of people cannot be justified.

seize (v.)
grab, grasp, clutch, grip, snatch
She seized the opportunity that came her way.

seldom (adv.)
rarely, infrequently, not often, hardly ever, very occasionally
We seldom see our friends after we shifted to a new city.

semblance (n.)
appearance, image, likeness, resemblance, bearing, aspect, mien, exterior, front, face

There is a semblance of quiet in the colony.

sensational (adj.)
exciting, stimulating, electrifying, thrilling, stirring, breath-taking, amazing, staggering, mind-boggling
News nowadays focuses on sensational topics to increase TRP.

sensitive (adj.)
delicate, tender, sore, susceptible
My skin is still sensitive.

sensual (adj.)
physical, appetitive, carnal, bodily, fleshly, erotic, sexual
Her sensual dance won her many admirers.

sentimental (adj.)
emotional, sympathetic, compassionate, tender
He is sentimental about his family.

seraphic (adj.)
angelic, celestial, divine, heavenly, sublime, empyrean, ethereal
Her seraphic personality could not be ignored.

serene (adj.)
peaceful, tranquil, calm, pacific, restful, idyllic, quiet
The serene atmosphere of the mountains is irresistible.

servile (adj.)
submissive, subservient, menial, slavish, grovelling, obsequious, subservient
His servile ways led to his gradual success.

severe (adj.)
strict, harsh, rigorous, hard, stony, unbending, rigid, pitiless
He was meted with severe treatment in the hostel.

shake (v.)
quiver, quake, shudder, waver, tremble, shiver
She was shaking with fear after seeing the movie.

sham (n.)
fake, fraud, hoax, humbug, pretense
The promises of the parties before the elections are a sham.

shatter (v.)
disintegrate, smash, demolish, splinter, fragment, fracture
He shattered her heart by rejecting her love.

sheen (n.)
shine, gleam, polish, burnish, brightness, glow, glimmer, shimmer, glint, dazzle
This sheen is a product of the sunlight falling on the water.

shirk (v.)
avoid, evade, shun, dodge
He likes to shirk his responsibilities.

shoddy (adj.)
shabby, inferior, poor, rubbishy, cheap, mediocre, tawdry, trashy
I don't appreciate his shoddy work.

shortcoming (n.)
failure, defect, deficiency, weakness, drawback, imperfection, flaw
I can already visualise the shortcomings of this project.

shrewd (adj.)
clever, astute, cunning, acute, sharp, crafty, manipulative, calculative, foxy, wily
Shylock was thought to be a shrewd man.

shy (adj.)
diffident, coy, bashful, reserved, timid, meek, sheepish, timorous
Timothy is a shy girl, who wouldn't talk to anyone except her family.

significance (n.)
meaning, sense, signification, denotation, purport
He couldn't see the significance of water in the village.

simultaneous (adj.)
coincident, coinciding, concurrent
Their simultaneous exit from the hotel meant something.

sin (n.)
trespass, transgression, impiety, profanation, desecration, devilry, sacrilege, crime, misdeed
Jesus took upon himself all the sins of the mankind.

site (n.)
location, place, plot, spot, locale, area, milieu, position, situation
The site of construction would be finalised after the meeting.

skilful (adj.)
accomplished, adept, adroit, dexterous, expert, proficient, masterful,

talented, capable, qualified, experienced
His skilful hands did magic with the furniture.

slack (adj.)
careless, indolent, lax, lazy, idle, slothful, sluggish, lethargic
His slack ways were responsible for his failure in life.

slander (n. & v.)
defamation, calumny, misrepresentation, slur, vilification, libel, disparage, malign
His slander against me was not expected. (n.)
She slandered him, as he cheated on her. (v.)

slaughter (n.)
butchery, massacre, killing, bloodshed, carnage, extermination, execution, murder
They slaughtered her like they would have done to an animal.

slavery (n.)
enslavement, bondage, thraldom, servitude, serfdom, vassalage, subjugation
The colonised races had to give into the practice of slavery.

smolder (v.)
burn; seethe, simmer, chafe, fume, boil
We witnessed the fire that smoldered and destroyed everything.

smug (adj.)
self-satisfied, complacent, self-important, conceited
She is a bit too smug about the comforts and wealth that she has, and that would lead her with no friends.

snappish (adj.)
testy, petulant, peevish, irritable, touchy, irascible, quick-tempered, waspish
His snappish disposition does not go down well with people.

sneer (v.)
smirk, sniff, scorn, deride, mock
He sneers at other people's achievements.

snobbery (n.)
pretentiousness, hauteur, superciliousness, presumptuousness, pompousness, inflatedness, smugness
The snobbery of the rich is not a rare phenomenon.

snug (adj.)
cosy, comfortable, intimate, relaxing, warm, homely
She was quite snug at her sister's place.

soak (v.)
drench, saturate, wet, immerse
He soaked his clothes into the water for an hour.

soar (v.)
rise, fly, hover, float, hang
The glider soared over the hills, catching every updraught.

sob (v.)
cry, weep, blubber, whimper, wail
The parents sobbed after their son deserted them.

sociable (adj.)
friendly, affable, approachable, gregarious, outgoing, amicable, congenial, cordial
The sociable nature of the neighbours was a refreshing find.

solace (n.)
comfort, consolation, relief, balm, support
The only solace that she had after the death of her child was her dog, Chandler.

solidarity (n.)
unity, unanimity, unification, concordance, mutuality, camaraderie
The spirit of solidarity is necessary in the times of war.

solitude (n.)
solitariness, aloneness, isolation, seclusion
He greatly relishes his solitude whenever he gets it.

solo (adv.)
alone, unaccompanied, single
He went solo to the New Year party.

solve (v.)
disentangle, clarify, decipher, crack, resolve
Stephen Hawking was responsible for solving many scientific conundrums.

sombre (adj.)
gloomy, morose, morbid, melancholy, dismal, unhappy, serious, dolorous, mournful
Her sombre look drew a lot of attention.

somehow (adv.)
someway, in some way
Somehow we managed to get extra luggage on the plane.

sometimes (adv.)
occasionally, on occasion, off and on, at times
We would sometimes go to the beach to catch a break.

soon (adv.)
before long, presently, momentarily, shortly
They are soon going to leave for the airport.

sophisticated (adj.)
cultivated, cultured, refined, experienced, worldly, polished, elegant, urbane, suave
Their sophisticated manners have won them respect in the society.

spacious (adj.)
vast, large, extensive, enormous, ample, expansive, roomy, huge, sizeable, large, capacious, immense, voluminous
She had a spacious house, which could easily accommodate ten people.

spasmodic (adj.)
spasmodical, paroxysmal, convulsive, jerky, sudden
She had a spasmodic pain in her hand.

spearhead (v.)
launch, initiate, lead, pioneer, trailblaze, vanguard
Virginia Woolf spearheaded the feminist movement in literature.

spectacle (n.)
show, display, sight, performance, event, presentation, exhibition, demonstration, extravaganza, wonder
She made a spectacle outside the mall, when they denied her entry.

spectral (adj.)
ghostly, phantom, eerie, incorporeal, supernatural
Hamlet saw a spectral figure which resembled like his father and that triggered his revenge.

speculation (n.)
conjecture, guess, hypothesis, theory, guesswork, postulation, supposition
His speculations about them being criminals could also be gravely wrong.

spellbinding (adj.)
fascinating, enthralling,

captivating, enrapturing, bewitching, mesmerising
She gave the most spellbinding ballet performance of all times.

spineless (adj.)
weak, feeble, irresolute, weak-willed, indecisive, impotent, powerless, cowardly
She is a spineless woman, who wouldn't do anything that her husband doesn't approve of.

spoilsport (n.)
killjoy, damper
Why are you being such a spoilsport?

spontaneous (adj.)
unpremeditated, unplanned, impromptu, extemporaneous, unprepared, unrehearsed
Her spontaneous performance was better than others' planned ones.

sprightly (adj.)
lively, vivacious, animated, sportive, active, agile, energetic, playful, spirited
The sprightly ways of children are a joy to watch.

stability (n.)
steadiness, solidity, firmness, soundness, sturdiness, strength
No one can offer you the stability that your family can.

stagnant (adj.)
motionless, standing, still, immobile, flat
It can be said that any job no matter how interesting becomes stagnant after a point.

stain (n. & v.)
blot, mark, spot, blotch, smirch, speck
I saw a big stain on her shirt. (n.)
He has stained the household's name by robbing the bank. (v.)

stamina (n.)
ruggedness, vigour, robustness, indefatigability, energy, power, might, stalwartness
He has the stamina of giving two performances in a row.

stark (adv.)
completely, utterly, wholly, entirely, totally, fully, altogether, plainly, clearly

He was stark naked when he entered the room.

startling (adj.)
shocking, terrifying, frightening, astonishing, disturbing, unsettling, upsetting
The startling experience shook her badly.

stench (n.)
stink, reek, odour
The stench of rotten food is emanating from the kitchen.

stifle (v.)
suffocate, smother, choke, strangle, asphyxiate
The son stifled his mother for her wealth.

stigma (n.)
brand, mark, blot, stain, taint, blemish, blot
Widowhood is not the social stigma it used to be.

stimulating (adj.)
exciting, inspiring, arousing, stirring, animating
I cannot recall having spent a more stimulating evening in the theatre.

stratagem (n.)
trick, artifice, device, wile, ruse, plan, scheme, plot, manoeuvre, ploy, tactic
They employed several stratagems to win the competition.

strife (n.)
discord, disharmony, disagreement, conflict, rivalry, competition, contention, dispute, struggle
The family is divided by the strife of perennial property issues.

stubborn (adj.)
obstinate, unyielding, inflexible, intransigent, uncompromising, adamant, recalcitrant
His stubborn manner is not appreciated by others.

suave (adj.)
sophisticated, urbane, worldly, smooth, civilised, cultivated, polite, charming
A suave gentleman like him is not to be found these days.

subdue (v.)
suppress, control, overpower, dominate, bridle, tame
He subdued his opponent using his might.

subversion (n.)
overthrow, ruin, upheaval, inversion
The subversion of his argument by the opposition lawyer left him fuming.

succumb (v.)
yield, give up, surrender, submit, capitulate
The soldiers succumbed to the other nation's forces.

suddenly (adv.)
instantly, instantaneously, fleetingly, abruptly, swiftly
He started crying suddenly after he saw the picture of his mother.

suffering (n.)
pain, agony, distress, misery, affliction, hardship, torment, tribulation, trial
She was undoubtedly suffering post her husband's death.

summit (n.)
peak, top, apex, acme, pinnacle, zenith
There was nothing left for him to achieve in the company after he had touched the summit of excellence.

sumptuous (adj.)
expensive, extravagant, lavish, luxurious, opulent, palatial, royal, majestic, regal, magnificent
I cannot forget the sumptuous meal they served us at the wedding.

supposedly (adv.)
allegedly, theoretically, hypothetically, presumably
She is supposedly a brilliant make-up artist.

suspect (v.)
disbelieve, doubt, mistrust, distrust
The police suspect the servant to be the killer of the old man.

systematic (adj.)
organised, planned, methodical, orderly, well-organised, standarised
The way they do things at the airport is quite systematic.

□

taboo (adj.)
anathema, forbidden, interdicted, prohibited, illegal, illicit
The donning of Western clothes is a taboo topic in our traditional household.

taciturn (adj.)
silent, uncommunicative, mute, reticent, reserved, quiet
He is a taciturn person, who would only speak when he chooses to.

tactful (adj.)
discreet, diplomatic, clever, prudent, careful
Most of the employees in our company are tactful.

tale (n.)
story, narrative, account, chronicle, narration
The tales of Panchatantra are a favourite with children.

talented (adj.)
gifted, accomplished, skilled, masterful, dexterous, deft
Caroline is a really talented girl.

talkative (adj.)
garrulous, loquacious, verbose, wordy, chatty, talky
I cannot handle that talkative class.

tamper (v.)
interfere, meddle, intermeddle
He secretively tampered with the confidential data.

tantalise (v.)
tease, taunt, provoke, bait, tempt
He tantalised the child by giving him chocolate.

target (n.)
goal, object, objective, aim, end
They have set the target too high this time.

tarnish (v.)
sully, taint, blemish,

stain, blot, soil, defame, spoil, ruin, damage, dishonour
She tarnished the name of the community by doing what was clearly prohibited.

taunt (v. & n.)
tease, jeer, mock, deride, sneer, insult, ridicule
He was taunted by others on account of being fat. (v.)
People subjected her to several taunts. (n.)

tedious (adj.)
boring, endless, monotonous, unchanging, laborious, wearying, exhausting, fatiguing, tiresome
Hers is a tedious job of juggling between home and work.

temperamental (adj.)
moody, sensitive, touchy, hypersensitive, volatile, petulant, hotheaded, excitable
You should deal with her carefully, as she is a temperamental one.

tenable (adj.)
defensible, supportable, justifiable, viable, plausible, believable, credible, conceivable
The new scientist had shown that the old theory was no longer tenable.

terminate (v.)
stop, end, finish, cease, conclude, discontinue, drop, abort
After the meeting, they terminated Paul's contract.

terrify (v.)
alarm, frighten, scare, horrify, stun, petrify
The child was terrified after watching that horror movie.

terse (adj.)
concise, brief, short, compact, pithy, summary, crisp, curt
When asked by the principal, she gave a terse report of what had happened.

testify (v.)
state, assert, attest, say, affirm, declare, vouchsafe
The criminal's sister refused to testify at the last moment.

theft (n.)
robbery, stealing,

pilfering, filching, thievery, purloining, larceny
The robbers escaped after the theft.

therefore (adv.)
consequently, so, thus, hence
The students have stopped coming for the classes. Therefore, we are not conducting classes next semester.

thoroughly (adv.)
completely, downright, totally, entirely, wholly, fully
She thoroughly read the script of the play before rehearsal.

though (conj.)
although, while, albeit, granted, even if
Though it is a perfect fit, but I hate the design of the dress.

thrashing (n.)
beating, whipping, flogging, mauling, lashing, battering, pounding
He received a thrashing from his parents after he hit his sister.

threatening (adj.)
ominous, menacing, portentous, sinister, looming, minatory, intimidating
His threatening glance left me dumbfounded.

thrifty (adj.)
economical, parsimonious, frugal, penurious, niggardly, stingy, miserly
His is unbelievably thrifty when it comes to food.

thrilling (adj.)
exciting, stimulating, animating, electrifying, enlivening, stirring, striking, gripping, sensational, riveting
His thrilling performance blew everyone away.

thrust (v.)
push, shove, drive, force, impel, ram, prod, jostle
She thrust her way through the throng of people.

thug (n.)
hooligan, gangster, desperado, hoodlum, ruffian
He is an infamous thug of that part of the town.

timid (adj.)
shy, coy, bashful, diffident, timorous, fearful, mousy, scared, nervous, cowardly
She is a timid girl, who likes to keep to her own self.

tiny (adj.)
minute, minuscule, diminutive, small, little, miniature, micro, mini, slight, trifling, puny
He gifted her a tiny present on her birthday.

tirade (n.)
declamation, harangue, diatribe, outburst, onslaught
She unleashed her tirade about the misleading information in the newspaper.

tolerable (adj.)
bearable, supportable, allowable, endurable, sufferable
The cold weather in the Himalayas was hardly tolerable.

totalitarian (adj.)
absolutist, arbitrary, authoritarian, autocratic, dictatorial, undemocratic, oppressive, despotic, tyrannical
Democracy replaced totalitarian governments in some parts of the world.

touchstone (n.)
standard, yardstick, criterion, reference, benchmark, norm
Her teaching practice has been the touchstone for many.

tour (n.)
journey, trip, excursion, outing, expedition, voyage, peregrination
They went on a tour after so many years.

towering (adj.)
lofty, high, soaring, outstanding, elevated, imposing, gigantic, paramount, extraordinary
The towering economy of our country is a great sign.

trace (n.)
hint, intimation, sign, token, suggestion, touch, vestige, indication, mark, record, evidence, clue
There wasn't any trace of the intruders.

traditional (adj.)
customary, usual, routine, habitual, household, established, conventional, ritual
Their traditional outlook alarmed the others.

tragedy (n.)
catastrophe, calamity, disaster, misfortune, adversity, blow
Many scholars look at the modern life as a tragedy.

traitor (n.)
turncoat, quisling, betrayer, renegade
No one could see the traitor in him.

tranquil (adj.)
calm, serene, quiet, peaceful, smooth, relaxed, sedate, steady
He often thought back to the tranquil, sultry summer days of his youth.

transform (v.)
change, modify, transfigure, alter, transmute, metamorphose, convert
He transformed himself because of her love.

transgression (n.)
sin, trespass, offence, error, lapse, wrong, violation, misdemeanour, wrong-doing
Her transgression cannot be forgiven.

trenchant (adj.)
cutting, keen, acute, sharp, penetrating, incisive, biting, sarcastic, acerbic, vitriolic, acrimonious
The critics passed trenchant remarks about the author's work.

tribute (n.)
honour, homage, recognition, respect, testimonial, encomium, acknowledgement, acclaim, commendation, laudation
The world pays its tribute to Mahatma Gandhi every year.

triumph (n. & v.)
victory, conquest, success, achievement, accomplishment, ascendancy
The triumph of the Pandavas was anticipated. (n.)
The Pandavas triumphed over the Kauravas as expected. (v.)

true (adj.)
correct, truthful, faithful, literal, authentic, actual, genuine, right, valid, verified
He gave a true account of the situation.

trustworthy (adj.)
reliable, dependable, steadfast, loyal, faithful, honest
As far as I can gauge, she is not a trustworthy woman.

try (v.)
attempt, endeavour, seek, undertake, venture, strive
We tried to help him in every way possible.

typical (adj.)
representative, characteristic, conventional, normal, standard
His typical reaction to everything new is hatred.

□

ugly (adj.)
unattractive, unlovely, unsightly, hideous, grotesque
There was not an ugly person in all the throng.

ulterior (adj.)
hidden, concealed, covert, secret, unrevealed, private, personal, underlying, surreptitious
Iago had an ulterior motive behind showing Desdemona to Othello.

ultimately (adv.)
finally, at long last, in the end, fundamentally, essentially
She ultimately had to reveal the truth.

undergo (v.)
suffer, bear, endure, experience, withstand
She had to undergo a lot of pain to give birth.

undermine (v.)
disable, weaken, debilitate, threaten, sabotage, subvert, harm, impair
He undermined that man's capability.

understand (v.)
grasp, comprehend, see, perceive, discern, interpret, recognise, know
She tried to understand the suffering of her friend.

undoubtedly (adv.)
indubitably, indisputably, unquestionably, certainly, definitely, surely
She has undoubtedly been the best student in the class.

unity (n.)
unanimity, uniformity, consensus, concordance, accord, solidarity
The unity of these brothers is commendable.

universal (adj.)
prevailing, general,

worldwide, widespread, ubiquitous, omnipresent, unlimited, common
There are some universal facts that cannot be refuted.

upbeat (adj.)
positive, optimistic, sanguine, cheerful
Giselle has an upbeat attitude towards life.

upheaval (n.)
upset, unrest, commotion, disruption, disturbance, disorder, confusion, chaos
There have been many incidents of political upheavals.

uprising (n.)
rebellion, revolt, mutiny, revolution, coup
The uprising has to be stopped as soon as possible.

urge (v.)
press, push, drive, force
He could not control the urge to smoke.

urgent (adj.)
immediate, instant, imperative, pressing, compelling, vital, important, rush, emergency
This is an urgent matter that needs to be taken care of.

usefulness (n.)
utility, applicability, practicability, purposefulness, point, benefit, advantage, expediency, gain
The usefulness of this item is dubious.

utopia (n.)
paradise, heaven, ideal
She dreams of a Marxist utopia.

□

vacancy (n.)
emptiness, void, gap, lacuna, hiatus, blank, deficiency, opening, breach, vacuum
She felt the vacancy in her life after her child's death.

vagabond (n. & adj.)
gypsy, tramp, vagrant, rover, wanderer, migrant
The way he lives his life, he can be called a vagabond. (n.)
His vagabond ways are appalling for some. (adj.)

vague (adj.)
indefinite, imprecise, inexact, unclear, confused, unspecific, hazy, ambiguous, obscure
I had a vague idea about his plan.

vain (adj.)
proud, conceited, haughty, arrogant, boastful, egotistical, narcissistic
The way she tends to herself, she is surely a vain woman.

varied (adj.)
diverse, mixed, miscellaneous, assorted, heterogeneous
He has such varied taste in movies.

vast (adj.)
infinite, unlimited, unbounded, endless, enormous, huge, tremendous
There is a vast gap between the different classes in society.

veiled (adj.)
concealed, hidden, masked, unrevealed, covert, disguised, secret
There is a veiled threat in the way he said those words.

venerate (v.)
respect, honour, esteem, revere, worship
They venerated him for his achievements in the area.

vengeance (n.)
revenge, retaliation, retribution
Hamlet's vengeance for his father seemed to be justifiable.

verbal (adj.)
spoken, oral, vocal, said, uttered, conversational
They had a verbal agreement about the work they were supposed to do.

verge (n.)
edge, border, boundary, margin, brink, threshold, brim
He was at the verge of being a lunatic.

very (adv.)
extremely, truly, exceedingly, greatly, acutely, absolutely, completely, totally
She was very attracted to that man.

vicarious (adj.)
surrogate, indirect
She used to derive vicarious pleasure out of others' lives.

vice (n.)
immorality, corruption, evil, depravity, villainy, venality, profligacy, sin
The Bible mentions numerous vices that mankind could suffer from.

visible (adj.)
seeable, perceivable, perceptible, discernible, detectable, discoverable, noticeable
We saw a visible change in his persona after he returned.

vivid (adj.)
intense, strong, fresh, bright, dazzling, colourful, glowing
She has a vivid imagination vis-à-vis her sartorial sense.

voluntarily (adv.)
freely, willingly, spontaneously, intentionally, purposely, deliberately
Parents voluntarily gave up their desires for their children's sake.

voracious (adj.)
insatiable, gluttonous, ravenous, rapacious, hoggish, devouring, avaricious, unquenchable, enormous
He had a voracious appetite for books.

vulgar (adj.)

indelicate, boorish, uncultivated, unrefined, inelegant, uncouth, coarse

His vulgar manners are seen with consternation everywhere he goes.

vulnerable (adj.)

exposed, weak, sensitive, unprotected, unguarded, helpless

She is in a vulnerable state at the moment.

□

wander (v.)
walk, go, roam, rove, stray, ramble, stroll, saunter, meander
All of us wandered about the forest in the day.

wanting (adj.)
deficient, inadequate, insufficient, unsatisfying, inferior, shoddy, flawed, imperfect
These machines were found wanting after they were tested for durability.

wanton (adj.)
immoral, dissolute, dissipated, depraved, promiscuous, lustful, licentious, wild, libidinous, lascivious
He is an infamously wanton man.

warmly (adv.)
affectionately, tenderly, fondly, lovingly
She warmly welcomed her guests.

warn (v.)
caution, advise, notify, inform, alert,
They had been warned about the cyclone. Even then they did not vacate their house.

wary (adj.)
cautious, careful, circumspect, prudent, watchful, vigilant
She has to be wary of that man and his unclear intentions.

wasteful (adj.)
extravagant, spendthrift, lavish, improvident, uneconomical
His investment in those shares was a wasteful endeavour.

weakness (n.)
feebleness, frailty, fragility, vulnerability, infirmity
She was clearly his weakness.

wheedle (v.)
coax, cajole, charm, beguile, persuade
She wheedled him into buying her jewellery.

wicked (adj.)
evil, bad, immoral, unprincipled, sinful, impious, satanic, demonic, accursed
He is a wicked man for killing his son.

wily (adj.)
shrewd, cunning, crafty, sly, guileful, foxy, shifty, scheming, plotting, calculating, deceitful
He is a wily player at gambling.

wise (adj.)
sagacious, judicious, reasonable, prudent, sensible, insightful, sapient, discerning, perceptive, intelligent
Sages are presumed to be wise.

witty (adj.)
ingenious, subtle, clever, sarcastic, piquant, humorous, comical, amusing, funny
His witty take on politics made his famous.

woe (n.)
hardship, adversity, misery, tribulation, calamity, trial, grief, desolation, melancholy, misfortune
The family was constantly plagued by woe.

wreck (v.)
destroy, ruin, devastate, demolish, shatter
He wrecked the lives of his family members.

☐

yearn (v.)

long, pine, ache, itch, hunger, crave, desire, wish

I have always yearned to see the Himalayas.

yell (v.)

shout, scream, bellow, howl

He yelled at his wife for serving him cold food.

yet (adv.)

as yet, till now, hitherto, still

The train has not yet entered the station.

yield (v.)

surrender, give up, submit capitulate, succumb

The army yielded to the attacks of the rival party.

□

zealot (n.)
fanatic, extremist, radical
A party of zealots has been secretively formed to respond to the attack.

zenith (n.)
summit, acme, apex, vertex, top, peak, pinnacle
She reached the zenith of her beauty, and then that beauty gradually started fading away.

zest (n.)
eagerness, zeal, exuberance, appetite, interest, enthusiasm, hunger
One should learn from his zest for life.

□

Abbreviations

n. – noun
v. – verb
adj. – adjective
adv. – adverb

conj. – conjunction
prep. – preposition

□□□